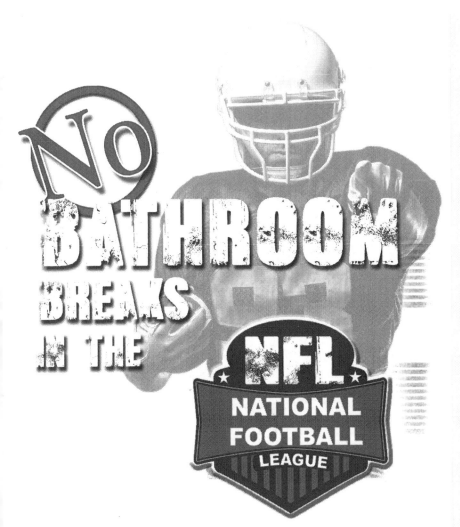

No BATHROOM BREAKS IN THE NFL

NATIONAL FOOTBALL LEAGUE

Published in collaboration with
Fortitude Graphic Design and Printing and Season Press
Cover and book design by Sean Hollins
Back cover photo of Jason Babin by Simon Swee
Back cover photo of Matthew R. Cooper by Deborah McCaw

For information regarding this book, bulk discounts or speaking engagements please contact Matthew R. Cooper at mattcooper@scsck.com or visit: www.scrafoundation.org

No Bathroom Breaks in the NFL: What it Takes to Play in Today's National Football League/ Babin, Jason and Cooper, Matthew- Non-fiction
p.cm

1. Sports-Football 2. National Football League-Players
3. Memoir-Jason Babin

Library of Congress Control Number:
2016953282

ISBN-10: 0-9977136-1-5
ISBN-13: 978-0-9977136-1-9

Printed in the United States of America

FIRST EDITION
10 9 8 7 6 5 4 3 2 1

In Memoriam

To Jim Babin, a wonderful man
October 29, 1957 – May 1, 2016

Table of Contents

PREFACE

So who doesn't like football? In 2015, Super Bowl XLIX (49) became the most watched American television program in United States history with an audience of approximately 170 million. A popular television show is lucky to draw 10 million viewers. While a highly anticipated news expose may draw 17 million viewers, the National Football League ranks Number One on five networks–it even has its own network! According to Neilson ratings, 80% of all television households will tune in at some point during the regular football season.

The Super Bowl has become an unofficial American National Holiday. After Thanksgiving, the Super Bowl is the largest day for U.S. food consumption. Months after the Super Bowl, the National Basketball Association (NBA) and the National Hockey League (NHL), are at the height of their playoffs. Yet, most sports television and radio programs commentators spend more time talking about the past NFL season, the draft, and the upcoming year.

Some fans love the game so much that they often refer to teams as "our team", and unofficially include themselves with statements such as, "Who are we playing this week?" and "We practiced well this week." More commonly are those on the periphery who enjoy a game or parts of games on a Sunday, Monday or Thursday night, and others who show their love and competitiveness as one of more than 33 million participants through fantasy football leagues and office pools.

The National Football League is exciting, and has some very entertaining characters. The League has just the right amount of teams, thirty-two. A team's season has just the right amount of games, sixteen. There is a playoff system that keeps the season moving from the suspense and excitement to a climatic finish. But, just who are the players? What are their lives like from their commute to work to weekly preparations? What are their diets and exercise regiments? What do they do the morning of a game?

Do they eat donuts before a game? Do they wear a new jersey for every game? Do they exchange memorabilia, slack off during the off-season, goof off with fellow players, or trash talk referees…or opposing players?

What is it really like to be a gladiator in the NFL? Are they bigger, faster, stronger, world-class athletes, Prima Donnas of society, or just like the rest of us? Are they humble gladiators with God-given talent who appreciate every moment in the League, or are they real butt heads?

Are they us?

This is a behind-the-scenes view of what it's really like to be a player in the National Football League. There have been salacious sex-driven stories and drug tale books, which feature some of the scandals in players' lives. This is not that book. This is a fascinating and enlightening story of the minutiae you have often wondered, but did not know who to ask. It will solidify your love, and give you new respect for the NFL and its players.

More than 100 million people are either fans, or among those who wonder what all the fuss is all about. Curiosity is a dominant human characteristic, and you the reader, is who we aim to satisfy. In this book I share what I experienced in my more than thirteen years in the NFL, and insight to the details you may have been wondering about as you watch the game.

In most civilized societies, people generally wash their hands after relieving themselves in the bathroom. However, in the NFL, we are looking at young multi-millionaires. They are world-class athletes with all the money and perks of their desires at their disposals.

Do they not still conduct themselves in a manner commensurate with societal norms?

Do they wear flip-flops in the shower or run around barefoot through the locker room and shower where other guys have perhaps urinated in the drain?

Are there more beauty products in an NFL locker room than in your local beauty salon?

Do some of these gladiators, after all, apply lip balm before going to bed?

Is the game *really* so intense that players just urinate on themselves on the sidelines during the game? (No time to remove trousers or wash hands!)

How fascinating of a dichotomy between living in a mansion with every luxury, to the animalistic behavior of game day where there are no bathroom breaks in the NFL.

PART
1

Chapter One

LARRY, MOE AND CURLY

It was a brisk fall morning. The dew was dripping like honeysuckle from the damp, shaded leaves. The young men chose their dapper outfits with care and speculated the day's upcoming trials and tribulations. They are of an enlightened generation, full of caution, and circumspection.

The day before was full of endearing entanglements that required study and learning of one's character and past faux pas. It is the day after an outing on the Grid Iron and the gentlemen need to examine, study and focus to regroup for the next competitive squaring off with another organization within the League.

Stop! No more frivolities or flowery feel good words. This is a book about "Curly."

The story begins....

On the morning after a Sunday game, Curly rolls out of bed. It's about fifteen minutes before he can lumber into the kitchen to grab his glass of water with lemon and honey to re-hydrate.

He gets to the practice facility to review game film of the previous day along with his teammates. However, before the film even begins, he is put on notice that he is five minutes late. Being late will mean that the Kangaroo Court will impose a fine (a tax) on Curly. But that is just the beginning of his Kangaroo Court adventures this day.

As the film begins, the room erupts with great roaring laughter. Teammates flinch as Curly, is pancaked (knocked to his ass and driven into the turf) by the opposing 350-pound guard. The pain from that blow is what led to his tardiness. Not only does he have to physically reminisce the incident, he has to feel the full brunt of that event through the laughter and embarrassment bestowed upon him by his fellow teammates.

1

Curly saw his mistake while he watched the film. It was one of the biggest mistakes a defensive linemen can make. He stood upright and gave the guard all the leverage. While Curly stepped forward with his outside leg in midair, the guard surprised him and planted the pancake move that drove him to the ground. Normally, two sacks in a game were wonderful for Curly, but unfortunately, with the game loss the Kangaroo Court imposed a hefty fine for the embarrassment.

Let's rewind...

I can tell you what happened to Curly, because I've been Curly... Larry, and Moe during my life in the NFL. My name is Jason Babin. Depending upon the year you are reading this, I am one of the more seasoned and elder statesmen in the League.

I was born in 1980, in a small mid-western town in Southwest Michigan called Paw Paw. Folks in Michigan say, "It is a town so nice, they named it twice." While Paw Paw is a Village of around 3,000 people, some famous people have called Paw Paw home. Charlie Maxwell, an All-Star player with the Detroit Tigers calls Paw Paw home, as does Jerry Mitchell, a Tony Award-winning Broadway choreographer. Had I not made it into the NFL, it was my dream to become a Navy Seal. I need goals and an ability to turn my testosterone into positive activity.

There are many examples I drew upon in Paw Paw. I most admired Ted Major, a 1942 graduate of Paw Paw High School. He served in the U.S. Navy during World War II, and was a commissioned officer and Ensign on the USS Europa. In 1950, he was an officer aboard the USS Eldorado.

During the Korean War, Ted's assignment was to sneak onto the shores of North Korea and move inland to report how many Chinese came into the country. He and three other men snuck onto the shores of North Korea in a little boat. Paw Paw's own Ted Major (a Navy Seal before the Navy had Seals) set the bar for what Navy Seals would become.

As a fellow Paw Paw High School graduate, I also aimed to set a bar. I played in two Pro-Bowls (2010 and 2011) and was selected second team All-Pro. I attended and played football for Western Michigan University, and in 2003, I was second team All-American. I received the MAC Defensive Player of the Year and first team All-MAC–twice for each.

I am 6'2 ¾" and around 260 pounds. For a man my size I was blessed with extraordinary speed and quickness. Most NFL players note that the major significant difference between college and the NFL is the speed of the action, speed of the players, the extraordinary size, strength and fitness of the players, coupled with the extraordinary speed of the individuals and action along with the brute force and power.

In 2004, I was a first-round draft pick and my career has gone as follows:

2004-06- Houston Texans
2007-08-Seattle Seahawks
2008- Kansas City Chiefs
2009- Philadelphia Eagles
2010- the Tennessee Titans
2011-12- Philadelphia Eagles
2012-13-Jacksonville Jaguars
2014-15-New York Jets
2015- Baltimore Ravens
2015- Arizona Cardinals

As of 2014, I have had more than sixty-six sacks, with fourteen forced-fumbles. Individual statistics for a defensive end or outside line backer can be deceptive. While the Pro-Bowl selection might mean the fans are drawn to tackles, sacks and forced fumbles, it does not provide a complete and accurate reflection of how I feel about my performance during a game.

As a veteran, I have learned a thing or two, and have observed a million or so other things that make up the NFL and its players. I focus my daily activities, every day, at being a standout in the NFL. Personally, my life's goal is to be the best husband and father to my wife, Sara, and my children, Talan, Maddux and Bronson.

Leo Tolstoy, Frederick Douglass and other writers throughout history detail how the average person obsessed with putting food on the family's table. Food was an obsession because it was so scarce and difficult to come by. In the 21st century, there is still an obsession with food among many. For many in the world, it is still a daily task to provide food for one's table.

For nearly a decade, three nights a week, I sleep in a Hyperbaric Chamber. During training camp and the regular season, I felt fine. But on the day off or before practice, I am in the training room getting massages and treating bruises, cuts and scraps. Preventative care and proper maintenance has been my secret to maintaining health.

The master, Leo Tolstoy wrote out of (I believe) a sense of boredom. The upper class did not need to work on a daily basis to put food on their family's table. In fact, the most demanding "work" he did (as he had servants) was to gather his own firewood for the day. And that wood was from what others had previously gathered for him.

I am of the most extreme physically aggressive player on the field. The coaches I love most are like Jim Washburn, who have allowed me to be me–aggressive, fast-paced, violent, and active– and to create plays. To do so, I need proper nutrition, hydration and muscular development, stretching, flexibility and mental preparedness.

I often tell players to prepare mentally. It truly means something to practice mentally what you are supposed to do for a particular play. Mental reps are real.

Practice facilities, player socialization and fraternization. Each team spends approximately $140 million a year on player salaries alone. If a team desires to relocate to another city, they are looking at a bill of about half a billion dollars from the league for the costs associated with the relocation.

Aside from the salaries, what are the perks and provisions provided for their players? There are ten practice squad players per team, fifty-three active players, and forty-six players allowed per game. With a salary cap limit on player salaries and a limit on the number of players allowed per team, with such parity, how do teams come to dominate and other teams falter and flail?

I understand that millions upon millions of people are fans of the National Football League and follow the players. More than 100 million people watch its championship game. I understand how people love to feel a part of something positive and big. But fans don't see everything.

Back to the story...

After the film meeting where Curly was heckled for his 350-pound sacking, he was approached by a veteran and advised of his fines associated with the pancaking, and the tardiness. At that moment, Curly's mind flashed ahead to the next day when the Federal Express package would arrive with his fines from the NFL. Curly was not penalized for horse collaring, as it was done within the legal zone and on a legal play.

Surely the NFL and its Kangaroo Court would impose fines. A typical active player could be fined between $10,000-$150,000 a year by the NFL. Some players or teams will have fines that require another zero added to the end of that figure.

Chapter
Two

KANGAROO COURTS
Where Do The Players Fit In?

In the early 1900's football was almost outlawed. Ultimately, eighteen people died playing football in 1905. The *Chicago Tribune* called the game of football the "death harvest." Many schools abandoned the game all together. The 12th man on the field was known as "death." Fortunately, President Theodore Roosevelt saved it. Roosevelt and the reformers worked hard to develop ways to get the brutality out of the game.

One of the ways was the movement toward making the forward pass legal. Prior to that, it was an illegal move. The Eastern Elite referenced the forward pass as a "trick play" – something left for the sissies. At the time, the forward pass was not only illegal, but the ball was not conducive to throwing tight spirals. The balls were melon balls that flew like ducks. Boomer Esiason said they were like, "a weighted basketball with laces."

By 1913, the League was exposed to what has become known as the West Coast Offense, when Notre Dame and Knute Rockne beat Army 35 to 13. While Knute did not invent the forward pass, he sure introduced its acceptance into the future. The NFL was formed in 1920 as the American Professional Football Association. It became known as the National Football League in 1923.

With the continued acceptance and precision of the forward pass, it meant that the game was never over until it was over. The genesis of the Hail Mary pass was in a game where Roger Staubach and the Cowboys trounced the Minnesota Vikings with only 32 seconds left in the game, with a long pass to Drew Pearson. While the ball was in the air, Roger Staubach actually prayed the Hail Mary until the touchdown was complete.

Since then, Hail Mary has been continuously used in the NFL as well as in politics by President Obama and War Commander, H. Norman Schwarzkopf, Jr., with his frequent use of the term during the Persian Gulf War.

Today, there are thirty-two teams in the League. They are capable of extreme and veracious violence. The game itself is physically and mentally demanding and taxing. Each team has fifty-three players on a roster who are the most elite athletes in the world. While there are fifty-three players on a roster, only forty-six are activated for each game. Each team has ten practice squad players.

Coaching staffs consists of one head coach and typically between twenty to twenty-five assistant coaches and training staff. Management consists of the owner/chairman/CEO, president, general manager, and seven to fifteen directors. On top of that add on equipment managers and ball boys. These "players" make sure that the players have everything from liquid on the sideline to domestic violence programs.

How do teams function with fifty-three testosterone-driven Prima Donnas? Many people refer to the way the NFL and its commissioner conduct business toward the players as a Kangaroo Court. However, in this chapter, Kangaroo Court is what exists among the players.

The players on the team run the locker room. None of it can function in a productive manner if not policed and put into practice by the players. Football in America has gone from being a game of brutality and death to one of speed, precision, strength and mental gamesmanship. While brutality and violent collisions still exist, the game is private through its extreme mental and physical requirements to gain admission.

The game's success is not only due to the rule of the NFL Commissioner, but how the players themselves police themselves and protect the shield. Kangaroo Courts on teams are an essential part of the hierarchy of the organization. It gives the players ownership. Responsibility is undertaken and ownership is what provides the ability for success.

Generally, on teams there are numerous courts divided among the coaches of different positions such as quarterback, running back, tight-end, offensive line, receiver, linebacker, secondary, defensive lineman, strength and conditioning, and special team coaches. These are generally the group breakdowns for practice drills, stretching and game review and study.

There is generally a hierarchy of the players within these groups and the veterans generally serve as the judge, jury, and executioner for the determination of violations and the assessment of penalties. Close relationships develop within these groups. Even though these are your competitors in one sense, a brotherhood with very close bonds are developed, especially among the players and those who share their position.

Players do not spend nearly as much time with the head coach as they do with the assistant coaches. The players' court system allows for the cementing of the bonds of all these relationships.

Earlier in the book, Curly was being accessed a fine for being pancaked. It is important to perform well and not cause embarrassment. Such a violation allows for certain camaraderie among the players, and at the same time accountability. This allows for the implementation of change and learning, as well as the infusion of comedy and the lowering of stress in a very serious and demanding situation. Curly was not just being laughed at. His brothers in arms were laughing with him.

Players are like family members. They have each other's backs and work with one another through serious times and comedic times. Being pancaked generally will cause a fine of around $500. Curly's lateness will probably cost him another $50-$100 depending on how late he was and what took place in his absence.

The more serious violations would involve a situation where Curly is off sides on a play where Moe miraculously intercepted the pass. Because Curly was off sides, the interception is negated. Generally, if the penalty negates a turnover, a player is looking at an assessment of around $1,000.

After a Sunday game, the various positions generally meet within their groups Monday morning as they have Tuesdays off. Normally on Monday mornings, a nice way of recovering from the game on Sunday is to begin the week by watching film. Not only does it allow for a recovery, but also it's an efficient effective use of Monday morning to not have something too physical, and to begin the week by reviewing the performance of the day before.

It is during this film review that most of the team Kangaroo Court violations are determined and assessed. Typically by Friday of that week, the fines need to have been paid. Obviously, one wonders what happens to the Kangaroo Court money. Larry, Curly and Moe need to eat and drink. They want their beverages cold and coffee hot. An NFL team is all about finances and logistics.

Typically, the players provide for the refrigerators or Keurigs that provide the little extra perks for team meetings, as well as snacks and incidentals. Kangaroo Court money generally pays for these extras. Also, generally rookies get hit with buying big dinners. Sometimes, veterans will help out the rookies, as well as Kangaroo Court money, to help pay for these extravagant meals. Each week money comes in there are always ways for it to be spent.

One way Kangaroo Court funds are used are during away games. If a team is playing in London they may spend the night after the game in London. During the week in London, the team is not allowed to go out during the week. After the game and a night in London, some Kangaroo Court funds are spent. Little extra perks such as dinners and parties are the best ways to spend the Kangaroo Court money as well.

Sometimes, there is a need to spend more money than is available. At those times, it is up to the judge, jury, and executioner to determine what it is they want to fine. From getting pancaked, causing a penalty that results in a negation of a turnover, to being late for a team meeting, are obvious causes for fines and assessments.

Put yourself in that leadership roll. You are the judge, jury and executioner. What do you want to impose and deal with to try to make a close bonding relationship? What do you want to do to diffuse the situation? What do you want to do to bring the players together and succeed and play towards winning a championship? We, after all, we are one and a lot like you.

Do you want to sit in a small room with five, ten, fifteen, twenty players and have someone constantly farting and gassing up the place? Do you want to feel and smell as though you are living in a pigsty? A player who is consistently without regard to the feelings of others, farts, and is regularly engaging in grotesque flatulence. BOOM, he will be fined $100 per fart. If he continues to think it's funny and becomes very stinky, BOOM, $500 a fart. The fines and dollars will fly until the negative activity is resolved.

Next, if you get knocked on your ass, BOOM, a $250 fine. If you miss a block you are supposed to make and are pancaked, the film does not lie. It shows that you just fell on top of the pile and BOOM you are hit with a $500 fine. Sometimes the court is team- wide and sometimes it is by the position. Sometimes it is all of the above.

The fines and penalties can be silly; but are all really quite serious because they are geared toward developing an organized team that allows the players to take ownership and police their own. From silly flatulence to the serious, to the extreme seriousness of fighting, it allows for ownership, accountability and family. The team will deal with incidents such as fighting.

The League will deal with their frivolous rules of whether your socks are pulled up high enough, but the true determination of what is important and what is policed, is from the players. They are the select few, the elite of the elite, the consummate professional of mind, body and spirit. They are who controls the team's success.

Many times, a lot is made of the brutality of the sport and the fights that take place. Truly, fights are rare. During training camp when there are ninety men on the team fighting for the few available slots, fights on the field will occur out of frustration and exhaustion.

Generally during camp, temperatures are hot–both emotionally and in Fahrenheit–and there is a tremendous amount of testosterone and competition. With the pressure and the aggression involved, there are sometimes fights that occur mostly out of frustration by players on the same team.

Most teams try to stop the scuffle before it develops into anything major. During camp, there will be many joint practices with other teams. These fights, among players from different teams, will occur mostly out of a testosterone-fueled rage and anger. These fights are also discouraged in that they only invite another potential for injury. Fights during season games are quite rare because of the potential consequence for injury and League action.

Players want to play the game, perform and win games. Coaches do not want fights as they create division and it's destructive. There is the general rule of: don't fight – if a fight breaks out, stay away. During practices, it is a waste of time, and in a game, it is a 15-yard penalty. Seldom will one see a fight occur in the locker room. It is all about policing their own, and the fact that the players own the locker room and want to have the backs of their teammates. Rarely do fights occur in a locker room as opposed to on the field.

On August 11, 2015, Geno Smith sustained a fractured jaw in the Jet's training camp locker room that resulted in him missing out on much of the season. Such an occurrence is rare. Not since 1974, when Clint Longley got into a fight with Roger Staubach, have we seen something of that nature from quarterbacks. Everything worked out well for the Cowboys and Roger Staubach, who went on to create history. In addition, getting rid of Longley resulted in the Cowboys getting Tony Dorsett.

It can sometimes be difficult with ninety men fighting, in many respects, competing to get on the team. The Geno Smith and Roger Staubach examples are entirely different from the scuffles and fighting that you see on the field of play. Generally, the fights off the field are over money or women, and are not associated with making the team.

Those fights are difficult to regulate.

Imagine what you would regulate in that role. Would it be players smacking the gum they are chewing during a team meeting, missing an important block, being off sides, or negating a turn over? It is all a give and take of trying to create a winning atmosphere. There is an important distinction that needs to be made between the activities regulated by the Court, as opposed to a team engaging in activities such as a bounty system.

The Kangaroo Court system is aimed at developing closeness and ownership of the locker room. It is almost a type of hazing; an activity that allows for the development of closer relationships and team fluidity. A bounty system does not play a role in either.

Chapter Three

FANTASY FOOTBALL

Fantasy Football has become known as a way that millions come together to become more intimately involved with the game of football. However, to most players in the NFL, the game of football (playing the game) can seem like a fantasy.

Look at most collegiate football players. By all appearances, most look like world-class athletes. They are gladiators of extreme physicality. They have speed, strength, and purely God-given size and talent. Why do some make it into the NFL and others of all similar appearances, strengths, talents and sometimes even more drive, do not?

Why do some have the most incredible muscular development and others can look like a Tom Brady combine photo and excel? How can one of the greatest quarterbacks of all time look like one of the biggest wet noodles at the combine and yet won five Super Bowls...and is still counting?

Others, no matter how hard they may work, train, and try to develop their skills, just do not have IT. Life at many levels is just not fair. Quite simply, no matter how hard or how strong of a desire and heart, most just will not make it in the NFL. Look at some of the family dynasties such as Archie, Peyton, and Eli Manning, the Golic family, and Clay Matthews and his family.

In their cases it could be Genetics vs. Drive and Ambition. Can one force himself into the League? Ala Todd Marovich and second overall pick, Ryan Leaf. Is it 10% luck, 10% skill, 25% guts and bravery and constitutional fortitude?

Obviously, one must have the heart, desire, and willingness to put forth the hard work and develop the genetics and God-given talents to actually make it in the League. During a discussion on the NFL network about draft busts, and ranking failures of the NFL draft, former NFL coach Jerry Glanville said that if you go bust in the National Football League, it is probably because you are afraid. In the National Football League, "they make everyone be a man." So, if coaches, league managers, and team owners have trouble figuring out how to make the team and succeed in the League, how are you suppose to select the players for your fantasy football league? Most importantly, do the players really even care?

At first, I would say that us players thought it was more of a fad and really didn't care about what was going on among the geeks and nerds who tear apart and analyze every aspect of our performance. We just want to play, succeed and win a championship. Statistics, while sometimes useful and valid, are for the fans. We feel we are part of a team wanting to win, and individual numbers do not translate into the final score.

League players are extremely competitive and want to have their team win. Even though fantasy football has become mainstream (and almost everyone now participates in some fashion or another) to me it is not the most productive use of my time. I work toward the continuation of my career in the NFL. I just do not have the time or energy to focus on something that is not as real as what is immediately in front of me–playing for my team to win. I fully understand the dynamics and the excitement that it provides for the fan. I do like that it is so popular among the fans. I want people to love the NFL and enjoy that many get passionate about what is going on.

My year is broken into the season and the preseason. I really do not have an off-season. Everything is geared toward my full time, everyday job of being an NFL player. There was a time when NFL players held other jobs. Now, being in the NFL is a full-time job. Unfortunately for the folks of the past, it was a matter of finances that dictated their ability to provide a commitment toward their team and career. The substantial financial reward players now receive only draws the extreme competitiveness of holding a position in the League.

Therefore, while there is financial ability to focus all of your effort into the realization of your dream (or fantasy), it does not allow the energy that is required and the expenditure to participate in anything that does not result in the advancement and continued achievement of your goals and career. The issue of whether we play fantasy football or not, is much different from whether or not we concern ourselves with disappointing fantasy football enthusiasts.

Obviously, it would seem that we should, in a politically correct world, say that we do not concern ourselves with fantasy football. However, we do understand the fans' involvement and want to provide them with the most positive experience of what we have to offer. With the enthusiasm that exists among the fans, we do have an awareness of the fantasy football pressures and need for performance.

Chapter Four

FIELDING A TEAM

So, Larry, Curly and Moe come into the team's locker room and provide the warmest greeting to the equipment manager: "Where are our helmets?"

"What do you mean your helmets?" says the equipment manager. "These helmets are not yours. Be sure to fill out the check-out sheets stating that you got a helmet."

What? Larry, Curly and Moe are millionaires in the most elite league in the world and guess what? If at the end of the season they do not return their helmets, they get charged for it!

At the beginning of camp, I am assigned a helmet for the year. If a chinstrap breaks, they will give me a new one. If a facemask has problems, they will repair it from their well-counted inventory of screws, nuts and bolts. If I give the helmet away and need another one, I get a bill.

League players generally can wear a helmet from any manufacturer they want, as long as it complies with the prescribed standards and rules set out by the NFL. However, from 1989 through 2013, Riddell was the only company whose name could appear on the helmet's front bumper. It is my understanding, that roughly one- third of the League's players do not use Riddell helmets, and chose instead to use one of its competitor's such as Schutt, Xenich or Rawlings. The front bumper plate of those helmets had to remain blank during the time Riddell had an exclusive agreement with the NFL.

Running an NFL team is all about finances and logistics. It is a business after all – business equipment and supplies. What are the finances of running any business? The employee (a player) cannot be allowed to have an unlimited supply of helmets. The owners buy the helmets, so if a player wants to keep it, the player owes money on the helmet, which typically costs $350. Why should the owner take a hit? Again, it's about finances and logistics.

At the beginning of each season, each player is provided with two home and two away game jerseys. Sure, if a jersey is torn or damaged beyond repair, I will not have to pay for that. However, if I want more jerseys–just like you, I pay the price the same you would. Now, think about how many of those jerseys you would want? How many people in your family want a jersey? How many jerseys do you keep for yourself?

Many players are into memorabilia. After many games you will see players swapping with players from the other team. Many players have their man caves, bars or simply have an understanding of their limited time within the League, and behave just as you would. Put yourself in their position. How appreciative are you to be a part of this elite League, and how fun it would be for you to obtain the memorabilia, mementoes, or souvenirs of your time here? Many players engage in the swapping of artifacts from players of other teams, as well as players from their own team.

I have had the privilege and honor of having a contract with Under Armour. My most recent contract allowed me to have around a $50,000 a year allotment of Under Armour merchandise and equipment. (Yes, this amount is taxable as income.) Yet, of course I am seen as having something given to me that I am more than willing to share with family, friends and youth leagues. That is a lot of equipment and I enjoy the privilege and opportunity to share with others.

Back in my hometown, of Paw Paw, Michigan, the Rocket Football/Pop Warner Football League is entirely self-sufficient. In a community such as Paw Paw, the youth program is not affiliated with a City, Village, Township, or County parks and recreation department. Programs in communities such as this throughout Michigan, and the country I am sure, are self-sufficient, unlike programs in more urban areas, which may be part of a parks and recreation department.

The Paw Paw Rocket Football program, through the efforts of myself, and a local attorney, Matt Cooper, worked to incorporate Paw Paw Rocket Football and obtain its 501(c)(3) charitable designation by the IRS. As a 501(c)(3) I have undertaken to include Paw Paw Rocket Football, Inc., in my charitable donations, as well partnership with the National Football League for donations to benefit the Paw Paw Rocket Football League. For years, it was my understanding that Rocket Football participants obtained their yearly equipment handouts through used grocery bags.

Through my contract with Under Armour, for many years the kids in Paw Paw Rocket Football, Inc., (sometimes more than 200 children a year) would receive their equipment in an Under Armour tote bag, along with new cleats specific to their fitting needs, as well as gloves, socks and other Under Armour accessories.

When there is a charitable organization like Paw Paw Rocket Football, Inc., as a 501(c)(3) the desire to give and improve it becomes contagious. For example, Mike Heistand worked with Mike Lounsbury at Lounsbury Excavating, to bring an awareness of the needs of Paw Paw Rocket Football. When they were demolishing the old football stadium at Kalamazoo College and were replacing the scoreboard, Mike Heistand received the necessary authority to take the old Kalamazoo College scoreboard and use it for the Paw Paw Rocket Football, Inc., field. The Paw Paw Rocket Football program now enjoys a collegiate scoreboard at their facility.

It has been a wonderful charitable endeavor to be involved with Paw Paw Rocket Football. In addition to Matt, others who have worked with me to help kids in the program include Lisa Hudson, Terri Williams, Rick Reo, Bobby Yarbrough, Tim Combs, David Leroy, Jeff Kreigh, Steve Barr, Ben Brousseau, Brad Newell, John Small, and Chris Tapper – just to name a few.

Under my agreement with Under Armour, I also get the shoes that I wear. I go through dozens of shoes a year–camp shoes, training shoes, and game shoes. Under Armour obviously makes them conducive to the requirements necessary for each team's appearance as it is an NFL rule that players have the same color shoes as their teammates. Most players have some kind of arrangement with a provider such as Under Armour, Nike, Adidas, etc., to provide some type of stipends for their shoes. However, many try to establish their own independence and will obtain their own type of footwear, or the teams have provisions to provide players with shoes.

Again, it's about finances and logistics. Owners are paying for the team's equipment. The owners want to have a flashy uniform that appeals to their fans and aids their players with comfort and their ability to perform. But of course the NFL, with its rules and a commissioner, obviously have a vested interest in how uniforms appear to the public and the way players conduct themselves. Believe it or not, there is quite an extensive NFL uniform policy that is incredibly strict. Players will be fined thousands, sometimes tens of thousands of dollars, for what may seem to be the silliest rule violation.

An example, Frank Gore was fined $10,500 for having his socks around his ankles. Well, the official NFL uniform rule (while it may be quite a bureaucratic mess that reads like a lawyer's case law analysis), is laid out for the players in a single-spaced, five page (small font) document. The League also provides the players with a diagram depicting a uniformed player that is one of the ideal appearances. For each violation, there is a diagram depicting the violation. The League's general rule is that "a player's appearance on the field conveys a message regarding the image of the League and directly affects the League's reputation and success."

In accordance with this rule, the NFL has laid out a broad overview of the rules players must follow.

- NFL Players are required to dress to the highest levels of professionalism.

- A Players appearance on the field conveys a message regarding the image of the League and directly affects the League's reputation and success.

- Accordingly, the NFL uniform and equipment policy was implemented primarily for player safety and to ensure that the game and its players are presented in a professional manner. For easy reference, please review the ten bullet points below to make sure that you are in compliance with the League's on-field dress code. Should you have additional questions, please direct them to your equipment manager or your club's lead uniform inspector. In addition, this section contains illustrations of the NFL Uniform and Equipment Rules and also includes a detailed description of the player uniform policy.

- Players are not permitted to wear bandanas, stockings, or other unapproved head wear anywhere on the field, even if such items are worn under the helmets.

- Headwear is part of the NFL Uniform Code. No commercial endorsement agreement entered into by a player can alter his obligations under the NFL Uniform Code. The only head wear (e.g.; caps) that the players are permitted to wear on the field is headwear provided by an NFL authorized supplier, currently New Era.

- Players pants must not be altered or cut in any way and must be pulled over the knee.

- The stockings wore by players must be white from the top of the shoes to mid-calf and an approved team color from mid-calf to the bottom of the pant leg, which is pulled down below the knee.

- Tape used on shoes and stockings must be black or white to match the selected dominate shoe choice of the club.

- The team jersey must be tucked in at the waist.

- Towels must be tucked into the front waist of the pants and are limited to a maximum of six inches wide and eight inches long.

- Shoulder pads and thigh and kneepads are mandatory equipment and must be worn by all players, except punters and kickers.

- Players must be examined by a club physician with a report submitted to the League office for approval, prior to wearing a non-standard/customized face mask.

- All points of a chin strap, whether there are two points or four points, must be fastened to the helmet prior to the snap. (Fine starts at $7,500.00).

- Clubs must obtain approval from the Football Operations Department before any new product can be used by one of their players in a game. The use of any product by a player during a game without prior League approval may subject the player and/or the club to significant fines if it is determined that the product violated NFL Rules.

The NFL posts the bulletins near the locker room doors. If violation is noticed during warm-ups, the player is made to fix the violation before game time.

So, the next time you are watching a game, and you see a player with his shirt cut off, that will be a fine as it is a violation of the policy. When you see a player with his socks pulled down below his calves that will be a fine. If a player gives a fan his jersey or helmet, well, the player will get a bill for that equipment.

At times you will see a player give a fan a football. That is generally a fine from the NFL of around $1,700. If the player throws the football into the stands, that could be a fine of $10,000. The NFL fines the player for the ball being thrown into the stands as it might cause injury or chaos for the crowd. Additionally, the player gets a bill from the team for the loss of the ball.

Finances and logistics. Imagine yourself running the program. There are costs and there is need for organization and the avoidance of chaos. There is a desire for cleanliness and neatness. There is a massive amount of responsibility and an army of personnel to play a game on Sunday.

PART 2

Chapter Five

THE SEASONS

Playing in the NFL is a full-time, yearlong job. Just as we all enjoy the seasons of summer, fall, winter and spring, life in the NFL also has its seasons– pre-season, season and off-season. Throughout those seasons, there is a common theme of satisfying the NFL requirements, managing and promoting media and fans.

On a personal level, there is constant maintenance of musculature development behind the individual health, mind, body and spirit. The priority however, is to focus on family–personal family and the team family. Throughout the year, there are subtle nuances to each season, in the management of diet, exercise, weight training, physicality, kids, wife, parents, family and friends, owners and coaches, and the NFL commissioner. It is all a balancing act to keep priorities straight.

Many of us work our jobs, provide for our families, and enjoy our time on this earth. At the same time, all of what we have worked for could be gone in an instant. Some have said that the NFL could stand for, "Not For Long". I ask you to relax, close your eyes, and imagine what you would do in the situations that I'm about to share.

I try to exemplify what it is to be a good adult. Therefore, you see many of us being professional and driven to achieve our goals. Sometimes you will see those who do not behave well and act out (just like people throughout society) who may not have had the greatest role models. Often, it is those players who struggle to maintain the accomplishments that they have achieved.

The current NFL player is, in a way, in the entertainment industry and has had the fortunate opportunity to acquire millions of dollars. Imagine what you would do with that type of wealth. It is easy to recall a day when NFL players were not rewarded financially. But as the game continued to grow, and has become the pinnacle of athletic entertainment for our society, its rewards too have grown.

I have been blessed to be in the NFL during a time when I do not have to work another job to make ends meet. In addition to the NFL, I own a cattle ranch in Texas. Our family (my wife, three sons, and parents) enjoys the outdoors and things like watching the herd grow and the cows give birth. If there is something we want, we can get it; whether it is a tractor with a front-end loader for the ranch, or a nice SUV. These opportunities are blessings that I count every day.

My body is a tool that allows me to participate, and my mind is highly relied upon to make good choices. While the NFL has been, in that sense, my "lottery win" it comes with great sacrifice, endurance and extreme physical costs. All of this is what makes the NFL player who he is, because on any given day, in a split second, it could all be gone. NFL careers are not that long. Depending on the position, the average number of years can fluctuate between three and twelve years.

I recently listened to an ESPN interview with Jimmy Johnson. Jimmy was preparing to go fishing the next day after he spent much of last week catching more than 120 lobsters. What a life! The point of the interview with Jimmy Johnson, also was about Chip Kelly's success (or lack thereof) in the NFL. Chip, formerly the coach for the Philadelphia Eagles and now coaching the San Fransisco 49ers, had a tremendously successful career coaching at the collegiate level. What is the difference between college and the NFL?

He succeeded in college, but struggled in the NFL through unfounded accusations concerning racial attitudes. It is more about his strictness. On the college level, Chip could tell someone to tie his shoes. The collegiate athlete is going to jump to the task and get their shoes tied. The NFL player is a man in the most elite League, and generally has millions of dollars. To have a coach tell him to "tie his shoes" is not the most effective way to deal with someone who feels that they are a man who does not need to be told to tie his shoes.

We see time and time again in the NFL that talent trumps character. While Chip had strict rules, he may not necessarily always have had a team comprised of the type of player with character that is conducive to that type of required behavior. Talent trumps character.

I have played in every stadium in the NFL. I believe that, based on the motivation of finances and logistics, it is pretty much cookie-cutter. Each team does not try to reinvent the wheel when it comes to managing a team and putting a roster together of a team to play in a game every week. What works has been developed, and what works, is being emulated by each team.

Examine any NFL team and you will see the army of people who work to pull off a game. It takes a multitude of experts in various areas to maintain the stadium, turf, showers, facilities, equipment– all of which are required to maintain an NFL team.

The basic structure of any team is essentially the same:

Owner
President
Vice-Chair
Membership Partners
General Manager/Assistant General Managers
Executive Vice-President of Public Affairs/Stadium Development
Executive Vice-President of Football Operations
Executive Vice-President and Chief Marketing Officer
Executive Vice-President and Chief Financial Officer
Executive Vice-President and General Manager
Chief Operating Officer
Executive Vice-President of Strategic Planning/Business Initiatives
Vice-presidents in sales and marketing
Consultants (from team historians to stadium management)
Administrative and executive assistants
Alumni affairs coordinators
Director of College Scouting (and numerous pro/college scouts)
Directors of Information Systems

In addition to these roles are service producers, multi-media specialists, production coordinators, graphic designers, archive designers, photographers, sales and marketing, stadium partnerships, corporate sales, charitable contributions, ticket sales and hospitality, sales of analytics and engagements, and probably 100 other positions that haven't been mentioned.

Players deal with front office staff for player tickets, managers, from ball boys to the personal that charge for helmets, to the person who maintains our personal equipment. It is a tremendous undertaking by numerous experts in their field to get us ready to play. While financially and logistically it is a cookie-cutter business, the differences come into play when dealing with people.

We all are individuals, and as human beings, we have distinct differences. Coaches, after all, are human beings and have their different philosophies, as well as offensive and defensive schemes. They have their different philosophies on how to manage and motivate men. From the littlest of examples, such as a head coach who does not swear and does not allow the use of cuss words in his presence (an obvious revenue for player fines), to a coach who throws the F-bomb around after every other word.

From motivation techniques to managerial styles, there can be vast differences like night and day. Coaches generally always want to win NOW, and GM's always seem to be building for the future. The NFL is made up of teams via a cookie-cutter business model comprised of human beings that vary greatly.

Therefore, while there is parity in finances and logistics, number of players and salaries, the different philosophies of the human beings involved result in how some teams are consistently better than others.

An off-season is a misnomer in that being a NFL player is a full-time job. To prepare for and play in the NFL is 24/7, 365 days a year. The pre-season consists of OTAs – Organized Team Activities, mini-camp, training camp (which has, as an extension, pre-season games). The season consists of sixteen regular season games (which should not ever be increased) and the playoffs leading to the Super Bowl.

Chapter Six

THE PRE-SEASON

I generally break the year down into the idea that I am always preparing and working my job as an NFL football player. What is the difference between the pre-season and the off- season? I do not live my life as though there is an off-season. Obviously, there is a time when we are not playing games. However, that does not affect my full-time job all that much.

It is important to realize how the NFL has changed over the years. For example, in 1975 the largest player in the NFL was Mean Joe Green of the Pittsburgh Steelers. He was 275 pounds. Today, the Pittsburgh Steelers alone have more than sixteen players who are well over 275 pounds. The linemen average between 350-400 pounds.

In comparison, in 1975 the Cincinnati Reds World Series Championship team had one player over 200 pounds. Now, most of the team members are over 200 pounds. In the 1970's players could smoke and even drink beer in the locker room. There are stories of bowls in the center of the locker room with whatever pain or speed drugs a player would want.

Furthermore, back in the 50's, 60's and 70's, players had to work regular jobs to supplement their ability to provide for their families. With the great financial rewards of today's NFL, comes great responsibility. The players are bigger, faster, stronger and the competition to get on a team is incredibly high. There are more players than ever coming out of the collegiate ranks and other football leagues who want to be in the NFL. There are only so many slots with thirty-two teams with a roster of fifty-three players.

My year basically revolves around when we have games. The official pre-season consists of OTAs (Organized Team Activities) mini-camps. In late May, the NFL conducts its draft and shortly thereafter in May or June, there is a mini-camp, an OTA that is strictly regulated by the NFL.

The original design for a mini-camp was to get the newly draft-ed players acclimated to the team's system, and to the teammates on his new team. Generally, veterans will come to mini-camps to acclimate themselves with the team and the newly acquired players. The mini-camps are generally from three to five days, and consist of the players wearing just shorts and jerseys. In fact, by contract, the players are not allowed to have any physical contact until well after three days into the training camps that come generally at the very end of July and into August.

The training camp invites ninety players to attend. Over the course of three to four weeks, that is reduced to the fifty-three-man roster. Within two to three weeks of training camp, there will be the start of the pre-season football game schedule. It always seems that one of the busiest, most hectic times of my year is July. It seems that the focus of June is on OTA's. While the mini-camp only lasts several days, there is the focus of preparing for and coming off the OTA, which is quite demanding.

With the start of training camp at the end of July, coming off of June through July, I am in my most hectic schedule of working out, dieting, getting proper nutrition and getting ready for camp. July is spent preparing for everything to be in order at home with my wife and children, because during training camp I am gone.

Soon thereafter, the season is underway. July is the last time I can be with my family before the season starts and my children start school and get ready for what their lives bring in the fall. Pre-Season football games and camp continues through August with the regular season starting at the end of August and into September. The season runs through the end of the year. The playoffs, Super Bowl and Pro-Bowl games take us through January and into February.

The daily activities of training camp are quite extensive. From early morning until late in the evening, we are working out, running plays, working in our groups, and watching film. Generally, Sunday would be an off day where we would normally fill most of the day in the training room.

It is interesting to think about how it is such a cookie-cutter operation and there is such parity among salary caps and the number of players on the roster, that parity is achieved, yet some teams are much more dominate than others. There are also differences in climate from one team to another. For example, the heat and humidity of Houston are brutal compared to the mild climate found in upstate New York.

Some teams engage in joint practices. Some teams are in camp for eight days, while other camps are just starting day one. The Collective Bargaining Agreement states that players cannot wear pads until the third practice of camp, so some teams are well underway as some are just getting started. One of the most important parts of camp for me has been the exercise of repetition, both physically and mentally.

Whether it is from rushing the passer to standing on the sidelines and engaging myself in mental reps, our bodies are conducive to the formulation of habit and routine. Whether it is from the simple aspect of waking at the same time every morning to the physical muscle memory of a certain maneuver, I like to engage in when rushing the passer–muscle memory and mental memory.

What I have found to be a truly beneficial exercise, is engaging myself in mental reps. While standing on the sidelines, I observe the activity that is occurring and mentally put myself through what is occurring in my position. Mental reps, mental reps, mental reps. I mentally engage in what is taking place and envision how I would react and play under that circumstance. You have to mentally see it and mentally believe it to be able to perform it when it is your opportunity.

At camp, all players are required to stay with the team in a hotel or university dorm. Generally, the team will have two floors of a hotel near the training facility. Players that have been in the League for more than four years are allowed to have their own room. Throughout our two floors, the team will post directives or flyers intended to help us with our daily needs from sleep, to getting our laundry done. These flyers provide tips and reminders to the players of the importance of sleep habits.

For example, a flyer will say:

- Lack of sleep can effect coordination, memory and energy.

- Close your eyes, relax all muscles and breathe.

- Get at least eight (8) hours/day; increasing this can improve alertness by 25%.
- Reading a book can help your body/mind relax and prepare for bed.

- No television within one (1) hour of bed, but soft music is okay.

- Your room should be dark, quiet, free of clutter and comfortable - covering your windows with dark fabric if necessary.

- Wear your sleep mask (provided by the team).

- No caffeine after lunch.

- Avoid alcohol near bedtime. Alcohol can disrupt your REM sleep.

- Avoid large meals within 1-2 hours of sleep.

- Showers/bath before bed will help you to relax.

- A twenty minute nap during the day can revitalize you, but any longer and you may be left feeling more tired and lethargic.

- Avoid sleeping pills, which contain "banned substances" and leave you feeling more tired in the morning.

Relating to directives during camp, there is constant contact with the media and fans. We are allowed to say whatever we want to the media. However, it is generally advised that you do not talk about other players. And when talking about yourself, you talk about the role that you can play for the team and how you hope you will be helpful to the team.

The media is at every practice. At camp, there are open practices where fans are allowed to come and watch. In addition, there are a lot of wives and player's children running around camp.

It can be quite a busy place with a lot of distractions. The team has a goal of eliminating distractions and trying to make it a day filled with routine as much as possible. They try to eliminate the chaos and provide us with as much as possible that will help with our focus. They provide everything from having an onsite barber shop, to teaching us how to deal with the constant attention of the media. They even provide postings, either in writing or verbal instructions during meetings, on ways to live your life and to generally conduct yourself. This includes media interaction, sleep habits, sexual relations and even how to treat your teammates.

I like to arrive a day or two before the commencement of camp. I say my good-byes to my family, fly to the destination, and stay in the hotel provided by the team. The team is excellent with the preparation of meals. There is a lot of food provided by the team as well as what you are able to get through the hotel. During camp, it is very important to me to stay hydrated.

Generally, I consume large amounts of Gatorade and water throughout the workouts and during down time. I am very proactive with the management of any type of injury. Whether it is bruising or any ache or pain, I am diligent about getting to the training room to have the bruising massaged and manipulated for a better recovery, and to prevent other injuries.

Every day, all day, we are either working out or learning our systems. The Kangaroo Court is in operation and we are developing relationships and building strong bonds among our teammates. It is important to get to know all of the players by name, as well as the staff, because we are working towards covering each other's backs and becoming a tight-knit group of a family working towards the common objective of winning a championship.

During camp I try to have as much contact as I can with my family. Imagine being separated from your family for weeks on end. This is the most crucial time for an NFL player because it is the period of time in which they are either on a team or released. The competition is fierce. It is mentally exhausting as well as physically draining. Therefore, it is very comforting to have a supportive family and know they are taken care of, and are active in their own lives.

The most important things for me at camp are maintaining my health, building my fitness, and learning my job. There is always something to learn in the NFL. The plays and schemes are complex and there can never be enough time spent in the film room. I thrive through camp maintaining a diet high in protein. I know some very physically fit players that consume 10,000 calories a day. Most importantly, the caloric intake is meals high in nutrition; not hot fudge sundaes and brownies.

I also know some players that are on a see-food diet. They see food and they eat it. I am very conscientious to only eat those things that have a nutritional value such as lean meats, vegetables, fruits, and grains. I am constantly developing musculature and maintaining overall health and fitness. It is a long season and our bodies endure an incredible pounding. I love to start my day out with an omelet, as eggs are great for protein and as much oatmeal and fruit as I desire.

Hydration is crucial. I am constantly hydrating and getting as much sleep as I am able. For years, a few nights a week, I sleep in a hyperbaric chamber. I am a firm believer in the benefits of sleeping in a chamber and what it does to my red and white blood cells. I believe the effect it has on brain swelling has been beneficial to me as well. It is my anti-aging secret. I have played consistently over 13 years in the NFL and am at the top level of the age bracket for NFL veterans. I completely attribute my success to fitness, diet, exercise, proper nutrition, and being constantly proactive concerning my injuries and injury prevention.

Throughout camp, there is regular contact with the media and fans. In fact, the media starts grading teams in May and continues to have us under a microscope through June, July, and August. Pundits start predicting who is going to win the Super Bowl while we are still playing pre-season games. Contact with fans continues as well. I regularly answer my fan mail. I started a Babin Fan Club to help specifically address fan inquiries. Further, I am a regular on Twitter and Instagram. I love the fans and I love having contact and providing them with information, as well as getting feedback from them.

In addition to my breakdown of the year, it is easy for my fans to follow my activities through regular posts on Twitter and Instagram. If it were not for the fans, I would not have the life that I do in the NFL. I have found that most players enjoy and appreciate their contact with the fans.

Fans ask interesting questions. One inquired about the plastic portable outhouses next to our practice fields. To them, it seemed odd that an NFL team would not have better accommodations. Before that question, I had never given it much thought (as my focus is on making the team). The fact that we have portable outhouses is something that is actually appreciated. They are convenient, and are not filthy, plastic outhouses for millionaire players.

I appreciate their existence, but rarely use them. Aside from the fact of hydration, one is not urinating that often during camp. In the blazing heat of camp, no one wants to be inside a port-a-john when other players may feel it would be a good break from camp to engage in some type of hi-jinx. Men are sometimes just older boys...even in the NFL.

I find camp very exhilarating and rewarding as I have been able to avoid being cut...or at least find my way on to another team. I see how hard other players work and notice how some guys have a tremendous amount of natural talent. It has to be very challenging to deal with the mental stress of being cut from the team. Aside from the sense of accomplishment and thrill of being an NFL player, it can be the difference between making a modest living or millions of dollars. Generally, the atmosphere is quite competitive, yet quite friendly among the players. The NFL and the teams do everything they can to help us work our way through getting on a team.

By September, the teams are cut down from the ninety invited to seventy-five players. The Saturday before Labor Day, teams are down to their fifty-three-man roster. Those cut have their hopes crushed and dreams shattered. These are tremendous people beyond being world-class athletes. They never give up, and continue to have hope of being picked up by another team or making it onto a team's practice squad.

Many contemplate whether they want to consider playing in the Canadian Football League (CFL), or the developing leagues in Europe, as well as the Arena Football League in the States. However, nothing competes with the status of the NFL, and nothing comes close. The NFL is every player's dream. Unfortunately, there are not enough slots for all of those interested.

During training camps, teams make all players afraid of being cut. Many organizations feel that it makes the players be the most competitive possible. During camp, as the cut deadlines approach, the cutting process is straight forward and really quite simple. During camp, the player gets a phone call and is told to report to the head coach's office. The player comes to the coach's office, sits down, and is told straight up that they are being cut from the team. One of the team employees escorts the player from the building after the player has been given an opportunity to retrieve his personal items from his locker.

This scenario plays out in any number of ways. A coach could say that the player has the toughness and work ethic, but they are just not playing well enough to make the team. Or, that they have a lack of speed, athletic ability, or intelligence. It is not about the fact they are not putting in the time to get to know the system or that they are not a good person.

It comes down to the fact there are other people on the team that the coach feels are better, and there is not enough room on the roster. In almost all situations, the matter is worked out in a professional cordial manner. Guys cut from camp know that they have the work ethic and brains to play football in the NFL, and that whatever they move on to after football, will be successful.

On the final cut day, it comes down to four o'clock. Who is in or out? Does a veteran get pushed out because his contract will cost more money than a young, cheaper talent who will fill the slot? Will it be a matter of finances and logistics, or finances trumping logisticalists? Many veterans who are cut for financial reasons will be able to get on another team. It is a constant balancing act between finances and logistics, and the desire to build a talented and hopefully winning football team.

Management is just a bunch of people. Walk down the aisles of a grocery store and look at all the products you have never purchased before or never even tried. People are all different and there are many different tastes. Players in the NFL are like products to management; it is like the grass is always greener syndrome. After the final fifty-three are decided, there is a lot of trading going on to fill the roster with players cut from other teams.

It is last minute and very high pressure; but you cannot worry about what you do not control. You have to keep the faith about your abilities. There has to be a mind set of what life is after football. The average NFL life span is around three years. Players have to have an idea of what they will be doing to put food on their family's table, other than football. The NFL can be like a lottery in that there is a lot of money available. However, just like with the lottery, winners have their lives ruined and end up bankrupt. The list of professional athletes that have made millions, even tens of millions, and have filed bankruptcy is enormous. In the NFL, there is the 80/20-rule. That is 20% of the players make 80% of the money.

As far as generalizations go that the public observes, there seems to be a lot of money available to NFL players. That issue involves a lot of thin ice in that the 80/20-rule applies, the lifespan of an average NFL player, and then the pitfalls associated with coming into a lot of money. All of the players have an understanding that there comes a time when you have to pack up and go. It is not a matter of if, but when a player has to move on to the next phase of their life.

It is gut wrenching to see a player's season end during a pre-season game or practice session. Veterans generally hate playing in a pre-season game when the brutality among the players trying to make the team is at its highest level. In fact, the manner in which the practices and pre-season games are conducted only presents a higher risk of needless injury. Training camp now is not like it was for the grey beards. The grey beards had two-a-days with full pads. They would spend days and weeks beating the crap out of each other.

Under the current CBA, we are much more limited with the amount of hitting and practices that we have a day. Players in today's camp take naps in the middle of the day. During practices, there may be music playing in the background. Yet, there are flashbacks to what the grey beards endured–if you messed up, coach made you run laps just like you did in Pop Warner Football.

Under our current contract, the practices at camp may involve less hitting. The trade off with the owners is the number of pre-season games required. When the players were negotiating their concerns under the CBA, they wanted to limit the amount of physical abuse their bodies endured during camp. This made it an opportune time for the owners to take advantage of the players to further line their own pockets by adding games. Whether pre-season or regular season, it is a money-making opportunity for the owners.

While the players tried to get away from the brutality of double days and were delighted to have them eliminated, the owners were able to use that to their advantage. They added pre-season games. The difference now comes down to the players wondering if it is different to have two pre-season games and eighteen regular season games, or four pre-season games and sixteen regular season games?

Once the NFL got to the number twenty, given the money it generates, the loss of revenue will never allow it to decease from twenty. There is no way it will ever be less than twenty, regardless of whether it is eighteen regular/two pre-season or sixteen and four. Depending upon the perspective–veteran versus a younger player trying to make it into the NFL–there is a vast difference of desire relating to whether or not there are four pre-season or two pre- season games.

While some players may not really have a chance at making the team, they certainly do not believe that. They are working their tails off. They do everything they are told and play at 110% during the pre-season action and working hard in the off-season programs. They practice hard and act like beasts during the pre-season games. If you are a veteran, is that someone you want to face? Veterans simply want to play in the regular season and collect their paycheck. These pre-season players want your job. The competition is fierce and they want as much opportunity to prove themselves.

Obviously, they want the four pre-season games. While a veteran under those circumstances would prefer two pre-season games, the trade off is that they have to have the eighteen regular season games, which is too much for their body. The trade off then becomes giving others the opportunity to prove themselves versus trying to preserve your own physical health and well-being with sixteen versus eighteen regular season games and the trade off being two or four pre-season.

Ideally, for a veteran or a regular player, we would like to see two pre-season games and sixteen regular season games; but that twenty threshold will never be reduced. So, while there is no more beating each other up like the grey beards, and no more double-days, now you have to continue to prove yourself in stiff competition. You must try not to get hurt, and stay healthy just to get to the regular season. It works either way from ownership's perspective. While there are totally different issues at play when examining double-days versus pre-season games, to joint practices for players, owners don't care, as long as they get twenty games. They get the gate and television time whether it is pre-season or regular season.

I believe that, since we are stuck on the twenty, four and sixteen is the best scenario. It works for veterans. No double-days. Limit play time in each pre-season games so there is exposure, but it is limited so there is less of a likelihood for injury and it allows for more joint practices. At the same time, it gives plenty of opportunity for the new players trying to make a team. Cutting it to two games eliminates half of the potential for the new players to get in some reps.

As a result of the incredible competition among the players, pre-season games can be a very exciting opportunity for the fans to view the NFL. During the season, the competition is between the teams. During the pre-season games, the competition between the teams still exist, however, you are watching players competing among themselves to make a team and are playing in a manner that is akin to a do or die scenario. Players are fighting for their lives in the NFL. Further, is it an opportunity to get a good view of the team's coaching staff and what their true ability as coaches are.

Think about it. There are ninety players on each team fighting for their spot on that roster. What is the difference between ninety on one sideline versus the ninety on the other sideline. There are one-hundred and eighty incredibly talented players playing at 110%. The true gauge of the better coach comes out and true. While they are trying to test various players, and test different schemes, it is still a good reflection of what the schemes and coaching abilities are when you look at the final score of a pre-season game.

Therefore, not only do you have fierce competition among the players trying to make it into the NFL, there is a competition among players to win the game, as well as the coaching staff to succeed in what they are trying to accomplish. When all of this is understood, the pre-season games no longer become a boring wait to get to the regular season and start participating in your office pools. For the players, it is the most important part of the season.

Nearly as many players that make the team (fifty-three), end their season (thirty-seven). Teams invite ninety guys to camp. It is all about leaving your guts on the field in the hopes of having the glory of making a team. These world-class athletes, whether they make the team or not, are playing for their careers.

Players under contract get paid in accordance with the terms of the contract, but what happens if you are cut? The regular season may begin in September, but these players that have been cut, have been working for nine months toward the goal of making it onto a team. Ninety players for thirty-two teams means 2,880 guys are invited to camp and are busting their butts. The NFL money is never guaranteed. If you make the team, you perform according to the contract and get your money or you are cut.

The 2,880 guys invited to camp are under contract. Generally, all players who attend an off-season workout or mini-camp (such as a rookie mini-camp or an OTA that you are invited to) receive approximately $150-$500 per day. Once training camp starts, invited players, whether drafted or not, get a per diem of around $900 per week that includes room and board.

The veterans, get around $1,600 per week. Those that make the team, then begin to get regular payments in seventeen weekly installments over the course of the regular season. These payments are all paid in accordance with the NFLPA contract provisions within the NFL CBA.

In the event you are lucky enough to make the fifty-three-man roster, you get paid in accordance with your contract. Most players make millions a year. The average veteran minimum is approximately one million. The rookie minimum is $390,000. If you are invited to be on the practice squad (remember each team is allowed ten men to be on the practice squad), the minimum under contract is $96,900 over the regular season. These minimum payments are good examples of the potential for stiff competition to make a roster.

Consider $390,000 versus $96,900 versus $0. It is important to understand that these are the minimums. There are practice squad players who may make around $300,000 a year, as a team can pay them to keep them a part of their roster/practice squad players so that some other team may not attempt to steal them away. Or, the team may want to be protecting them from other teams with the idea they may make a future roster spot on their squad. Just as these are minimum payments, League minimums, we also covered just the seventeen-week schedule and anything beyond that involves further minimum, pro rata payments. Further, most players have incentives for additional millions, particularly veterans and marquee players.

Also keep in mind that many of the signing bonuses are in the $100,000's to millions. Making a team is the difference between winning the lottery and throwing away your losing ticket; its literally tens of millions of dollars versus packing and going home. Now you can see how every play in a pre-season football game has meaning to a player trying to earn a spot on a roster. Every play is an opportunity for someone.

Think about the mental and physical exertion they are extending that may just result in a few thousand dollars and room and board for a few weeks. Think about that the next time you watch a pre-season football game and remember that this really doesn't matter.

Many incredible athletes are invited to camp and play in pre-season football games. It is a cold, hard business, and is all about raising the level of competition. The fans get exciting action if they view the pre-season games in the proper perspective. Owners get a gate and television dollars no matter the season. An eighteen game, full-blown regular season is just too taxing on players' bodies. Watch your four pre-season games and understand that you are seeing incredibly talented players who may try year after year to make a roster.

That competition is fierce and brutal. As a result of these issues, the NFL works toward the completion of a developmental league. While the NFL has developed an unspoken partnership with collegiate football that a player cannot come into the NFL until three years after high school, and has a pro hac developmental league with collegiate athletics, there is still an abundance of incredible talent vying for limited spots in the NFL.

From ownership's perspective there is an incredible over-abundance of cheap labor. Clearly, there is an advantage to ownership versus the perspective of an individual player. Think of that business motto for a moment if you are an owner or part of the NFL management. For that very reason, by its very nature, players will never have true bargaining power when negotiating with management.

Chapter Seven

THE NEW SEASON

The beginning of a new season is met with great exhilaration, anticipation, and relief. While training camp in today's era is easier than what the grey beards suffered through, it is still quite taxing. Veterans are just trying to stay healthy. Along with injury, age is another obstacle for allowing one to continue to be among the biggest, strongest and fastest athletes in the world. The clock is always ticking. The end of training camp starts a new beginning. A sense of great accomplishment is felt when you have made the team. However, the goals and aspirations grow exponentially. A new season is the beginning of a new year with new hopes and goals of winning a championship. There is no second place in the NFL. There is a sense of accomplishment in that days, weeks, and months have been spent forging a new team and building a new foundation. You are with a group of people from players to staff that you have spent more time with than your family, and are commencing on a new journey.

The new season is a new chapter in each player's Book of Life. Everyone within the organization works toward one common goal. It is quite an awe-inspiring feeling to be among a group of extremely high-achieving professionals who are working together with only one goal in mind. It has been a long road for everyone involved. While the players have extremely busy schedules, I do have a realization of what the staff endures. Every level from executive VP to the equipment manager is putting forth their highest effort in a professional manner. I think everyone finds it an honor and privilege to be a part of an NFL organization.

I have observed equipment managers who have to answer to all of us. They are there before anyone else gets to the facility to answer to the early risers, and are required to stay for those who like to stay after everyone else leaves. I am willing to bet that at times, the equipment manager is at the facility (whether during training camp or the season) between 5-6 a.m. and until 10-11 p.m.

We have all come a long way. We have an awareness of who is

going to be playing and who may have issues with the NFL. There are three different types of substance abuse tests that players are subject to. There is testing for two different types of drugs; street-type drugs and performance-enhancing type (PHT) drugs. For street drugs, we have three random tests between mini camp, the OTA in May or June, and the first week of training camp.

The performance enhancing tests can be one time, five times, ten times, randomly throughout the year. Before the season commences, there is a third test for HGH levels where they actually test our blood. These tests are obviously geared toward the NFL image issues as well as parity and player health and welfare.

***

In all of my years in the NFL, I believe I have experienced every type of living arrangement possible. During training camp we are in a hotel. Players with four or more years in the NFL get their own room. You can well imagine that having your own room provides many benefits over rooming with a fellow stinky, noisy slob of a roommate. During the season, I have lived with my family in our home in Houston and Jacksonville.

When I played for Seattle, Kansas City, Philadelphia, New York Jets, Baltimore, and Arizona, I either made arrangements to share living accommodations with other players, or I lived by myself. When my family is in our home and I live in a different city, I make arrangements through corporate services.

While the NFL has its business model down to finances and logistics, I have added caveats to that business motto to include finances, logistics and time. During the season, I simply do not have the time for maintaining the home, lawn care, general maintenance and cleaning gutters. When I am in another city, away from my home and my family, through corporate services I am able to select from a menu of items for the premises that I will be living in for generally a six-month period of time.

It is a full-service organization that allows me to pick and choose from cable, phone, fax, dining room, kitchen, sofas, beds and all the different types of furnishings that I may or may not want. Based on finances, logistics and time, I obviously choose locations near the hotel that we will be staying in for home games, which is close to the playing facility and practice facility. Regardless of whether I am living through corporate services, or at home with my family, the NFL requires great family sacrifice. Whether I am living with my family or not, I rarely see my wife and children during the season. The daily and weekly schedule is extraordinarily taxing on my ability to enjoy any time together.

There are always a lot of trade-offs that have to be considered when living in the thrill and excitement of a dream. The realization of what the NFL provides heightens a lot of the relationships that you build and the experiences that you have with your family.

My family has been able to experience things they never would have had it not been for my position in the NFL. Therefore, there are positive, as well as negative trade-offs in everything–including time with my family. Time, and the realization of dreams, is fortunately something we have chosen.

Veterans generally hate pre-season football games because we get knocked around by guys in their attempt to get into the League. These are guys who have everything to gain or nothing to lose. They have an opportunity to make millions, or go home. During an NFL pre-season game most of the guys on the field will not even make a roster. Fortunately, the roster will put the veterans out so that they can get reps, because under the current CBA they feel they are limited with the amount of practice time. Essentially, the teams and coaches use the pre-season games as a way of getting practice time in for the vets. It is a very peculiar mind set and motivation depending on the perspective and games observed.

My biggest "Wow" moment in the realization of what I was getting myself into, came when I was a freshman at Western Michigan University playing an away game in Wisconsin. There were more than 100,000 people in that stadium, and on the kick off, I was the wedge buster. The roar of 100,000 fans shook every nerve in me to the core. The adrenaline rush was like I had never felt before. I love being the gladiator in the arena. It is a ride and a wave that I want to ride as long as I can.

While a sacrifice of that is the time that I do not spend with my family, I know that it has allowed me the opportunity to provide my family with the time that we do have together, a higher quality of opportunity, time, and experiences than if I were not in the NFL. I may not take the time to mow the lawn at home, which is time away from my wife and children when we are together, I am able to take the time and cut hay with them at the cattle ranch.

Being in the NFL allows us to have the time together to work the cattle ranch.. I take every day as a blessing. I am constantly moving forward. Whether it is a play that went bust or an event that could have gone another way. Everything is always moving forward from the big picture to the minutia. I could be cut today. I could be hurt on the next play. The competition is fierce. I have always taken the approach of contemplating what are all the other defensive ends in the League doing at this moment.

What are my opponents doing? What am I doing at that moment that puts me ahead of what they are doing? My goal is to make this team and to help my team. Worrying about anything else, or doing anything else is a waste of energy. I practice being humble and focus to be helpful.

While I am living through corporate services, my family is back at our home. Our kids are in school and my wife is busy raising our children and taking care of everything else. Everything is everything. The responsibility that falls upon an NFL player's spouse is enormous. Enormous! My wife Sara is the best possible partner in life a man could wish for. She does everything for our family. She blessed us with three wonderful children, Talan, Maddux, and Bronson. Sara takes care of everything.

Once someone becomes so acclimated to air travel, the country really becomes small. It is easier for me to get, for example, from my home in Florida to Detroit, than it used to be when I was a kid in Paw Paw trying to drive to Detroit. As a result, it is really not that big of a deal for us to have family in Houston, a Texas Ranch, a family home in Jacksonville, Florida, and a home in Michigan near our Michigan family. We have typically tried to visit our family in Michigan during our country's Independence Day Holiday in July.

It is always fun to visit with family and old friends. A trip back to Paw Paw would not be complete without stopping at the LaCantina Ristorante and visiting with the Dacoba family. Having traveled the world, I can unequivocally state that it is the finest Italian Ristorante in the world. LaCantina has been serving up the best Italian food for over three generations.

The second generation is Norma Dacoba who is in her 90's and still works at the Ristorante daily. My other favorite stop in Paw Paw is the Oasis party store. It is a three-generation party store (Midwesterners refer to liquor/convenience stores as party stores). Beyond alcoholic beverages, the store specializes in pickled sausage, specialty candy, pop and snacks.

Having places all around the country, plays into my future planning of what life will be like after the League. I am of the belief that sound real estate investments are a good investment. So the family is secure, I have found comfortable arrangements near the training facility and stadium and a new season is under way. Yes, I am spending my evenings doing my own laundry and preparing my own meals…I am fully capable.

I know how to sort my clothes and turn on the washing machine. Meal preparation is not all that time consuming. If I am not eating at the training facility or at a restaurant, my diet is pretty simple between eggs, meat, fruit, vegetables and oatmeal. I stay away from processed foods and am focused on nutrition and hydration. Water and Gatorade are my staple.

Just Before Game Day
The immediacy of the next game really starts to take affect on a Friday evening before a Sunday home game. Even though a game is home, most NFL teams require their players to spend the night together Saturday night before the game. I have my own private, as well as public goals. Internally, I have always had the grandiose plans and ideas of playing in the NFL. It became my duty and my right. My stubbornness would not allow anything else.

So, moments before a game, it is a matter of gauging my mental preparedness toward balancing my focus toward my job, my duties, my responsibilities, and how I can help my team win. The exhilaration I felt at Western Michigan University playing at Wisconsin in front of 100,000 fans is still there…but I bury it. I make sure that it is something that I have become accustom to. I make it my normal so that it does not become a distraction. I realize there will be days in my post-NFL career that I will miss, and I will then take the opportunity to relish those moments.

But, before a game, I am focused on winning. I trust in my mental and physical preparations the week before. Everyone gets nervous and has butterflies; but, for most NFL players, that feeling is channeled into adrenalin to focus on performance, doing well, and helping your team win. The nervousness is about your performance, not worrying about failure. The preparation for the "immediate before a game checklist" begins on the Friday before a Sunday home game.

The life of an NFL player is very tightly scripted. An NFL player needs discipline and structure. During the season, a player's life, practically every aspect of it, becomes tightly regulated and scripted. Again, it comes down to finances, logistics and time. There is never enough time to prepare. There is always enough film and mental reps to take but the clock is ticking.

Generally, late afternoon on Saturday we arrive at a hotel in close proximity to the stadium. We are always aware of which hotel it is and it is generally the same one for each home game. Preparations and reservations are made well in advance...finances and logistics. As one can imagine, it is very important to get a good night sleep before a game. Teams generally encourage players, through polices, to get between eight-to-nine hours of sleep each night. Hydration for an NFL player is 24/7. Nutrition is equally important for providing the fuel necessary for our bodies to perform at their peak.

Just as in camp, players who have been in the League for more than four years are allowed to have their own rooms. Having your own room is very accommodating to get a good night's sleep. As you can imagine, there are players who snore, or are up late on the phone, watching TV, or just have poor hygiene. There are numerous factors that can affect your ability to get a good night sleep when you have to share a room with someone.

Much of Saturday is spent in meetings going over film, and final preparations of plays and anticipated responsibilities. I enjoy trying to slow things down, relaxing and allowing my mental reps to replay on occasion. There are team curfews. There is tight security guarding our private floors. The goal of ownership is that we are removed from any distractions and are allowed to get a good night sleep. Famous Green Bay Packer, Max McGee, caught the first touch down pass in Super Bowl history in 1967. At that time, and he had no idea that he would even be playing in the Super Bowl. The night before, he went out drinking and arrived the next morning in time to get suited up to play the game. Whether he was still intoxicated or hung over, it does not matter much. His performance was extraordinary in that he caught seven passes for 138 yards and had two touchdowns. The entire year before he caught only four passes. In the meantime, the days of spending the night out like Max McGee are over.

Note: Sadly, on October 20, 2007 Max met his tragic death when at age 75, he fell from the roof of his family's home while cleaning his gutters. The hero of Super Bowl I, died tragically cleaning his gutters.

On Sunday morning, the day of a home game, most teams schedule a time where all of the players will eat breakfast together. If the game is at one o'clock, this is the last major meal before the game. I like to eat an omelet with a lot of protein. Again, I stay away from processed foods. Anything with meat, beans, potatoes, or different kinds of vegetables suit me just fine. I try to provide the nutrition that my body will need for the entire game.

I am a big follower of the Glycemic index and am proactive in taking care of my body, organs and musculature. I focus on hydration 24/7 and make hydration a way of life. Immediately before a game is no different. It is important to prevent lean muscle mass from breaking down during the game, which could lead to injury. It is important that I maintain a good balance of protein, carbohydrates and sugars. Yes, we do drink Gatorade on the sidelines and I am hydrating constantly with water and Gatorade.

I believe for most players, the meal before the game is consistent with their thinking about nutrition and the health of their body. The days of players like Mike Golic eating donuts before a game are now the exception rather than the rule. (I think eating a donut before a game would reek havoc on my gut and intestines.) I notice that many players like to eat things like steak and eggs, hash browns and grits. Many will eat items such as a big bowl of oatmeal with fruit, potatoes and sausage. Standard foods these days are omelets, eggs, steak, sausage, oatmeal, fruit, potatoes, and a lot of water and Gatorade. Most players like to arrive at the stadium three to four hours before kick off. Home games are nice in that we have our own training rooms we are familiar with and film rooms if there are some last-minute issues we would like to address. Transportation from the hotel to the stadium is done through team shuttles, or players can drive their own cars from the hotel to the stadium. The teams are very good about helping players to the stadium and either transporting them back to the hotel or allowing us to simply leave from the stadium.

The teams in all respects are always very helpful to players when it comes to transportation. Teams are willing to help players 24/7 with whatever transportation needs that may arise. It is all a matter of trying to have a routine and maintaining structure. While most players arrive three-four hours before kickoff, if a game is scheduled for 1:15 p.m., the latest that some players are allowed to arrive at the stadium is around 11 a.m. The time before kickoff may seem like a long time away for some, for others, it may seem like there is not enough time.

Upon arriving at the stadium, the first thing a player does is walk through security and into the locker room. A player's locker is practically a double-closet size wooden structure with cubby's and the ability to hang your clothing. It is nothing like what most people associate with the word, locker, from our high school days. Shoulder pads are generally on a shelf above the closet.

There is a nice chair in front of the closet/locker, which has the game-day program. Hanging in the closet is one of your two fresh, clean jerseys and all the necessary equipment you will need for that day. Everything is clean, fresh and tidy. I imagine all players must feel quite special. We are like Superman with his suit hanging in front of us, or a gladiator or knight getting suited up.

I think that, when most players first get to their locker, they make a quick examination to make sure that all of their equipment is there. For some players, only upon their arrival do they know whether they are activated for that game. While there are fifty-three on a roster, only forty-six are activated for that game. The NFL only allows that amount as a means of trying to obtain parity among the teams. The thought is that there will be a competitive balance for a team that has a few injured players playing a fully healthy team. It also requires teams to be strategic in where they want to stack their strengths. I have always felt that it must be very mentally taxing to not find out until that moment whether you are activated or not for the game.

It seems quite brutal to find out whether you are suiting up for a game or not at the moment of arriving at the stadium just before the game. However, there may be a guy hurt from another position and that may change the coach's plan about who needs to be ready to play. After making sure that your equipment is there and you are activated for that game, most guys will go to the training room to get their ankles taped. I think practically everyone has his ankles taped in some fashion or another.

Many guys, after getting their ankles taped, will put on some light work out clothes and go out onto the field early to warm up and make sure the stretches feel good. There is never enough opportunity to stretch all of your muscles. There can never be too much stretching. At the pre-game warm ups, you will see guys in groups stretching together or just walking around the field doing their own thing. This is also an opportunity where you may commiserate with players from the other team.

This pre-game time is also the final opportunity to get whatever muscle you want massaged, or the players may get an injection. Throughout this time period, players are either in the training room, getting stretched on the field, or doing their own thing in the locker room. Many guys will actually read the game-day program or are reading newspapers or magazines.

Every single player has some type of pre-game ritual. I have noticed a lot of guys reading books, magazines, newspapers, or the Bible. There are guys who are calm, and there are guys who feel the need to do a lot of yelling to get hyped up. There are guys slapping each other and yelling at each other. There are guys just trying to be quiet as much as those that are trying to be all out rowdy. It is a group of men, that as much as they have so much in common, they have as many differences among them. It is really just a big group of older boys who want to go out and get dirty again.

One of the last things that you want to do before getting completely suited up is go to the bathroom. It is practically impossible to go to the bathroom once you have put on your pants, shoulder pads, and jersey. You don't see any zippers or flaps in Superman or Batman's suit; it's the same with us. Once suited up, the ability to remove clothes is difficult.

Yes, there have been players who have chosen to relieve themselves during a game on the sidelines. With the volumes of NFL rules and team manuals, nowhere does it mention the ability to have bathroom breaks in the NFL or to relieve one's self on the sidelines. (I hope I have not just spoiled it for future generations by giving the rule makers an idea for more sideline regulations.)

Is this a possible player behavior that does not have a specific rule or regulation? I guess it would be impossible to enforce as by the end of a game, most players are soaking wet with sweat, and peeing your pants is an action that goes completely undetected as it occurs. Finances, logistics and time. When in the heat of battle there is no time for bathroom breaks in the NFL.

In addition, most guys wear extremely tight jerseys so that the opponent does not have anything to grab. Putting your jersey on is quite an exhaustive endeavor and takes more than just yourself to do it. The training staff is very helpful. There are staff members willing to help you get dressed, with your taping, and with whatever other needs you may have. There is a wide array of medical staff from MDs, to trainers, to acupuncturists. There are professionals provided by the team to meet whatever needs you may have–medical as well as equipment needs.

The pre-game survey of the field helps determine what type of shoe players want to wear. The weather conditions will help you determine what type of gear you are going to need. Football is played in the extreme heat, to the severe bone-chilling cold. The old adage that "it never rains or snows on a basketball court or football field", is never more true than in the outdoor stadiums across our country.

Depending on ownership, there is a vast difference on the types of goodies on a centrally located table in the locker room. Generally, it is loaded with cookies, candies, chewing gum, and a variety of equipment such as extra arm sleeves, wrist bands, game socks, and gloves. Just as there are guys reading, relaxing, and getting rowdy, there are guys listening to a wide variety of music. Some play their music privately with their headphones and others have it blaring out for everyone to hear.

As the time to head out onto the field nears, this is when I imagine many guys are participating in matters that may provide them with an edge, or as some would refer to, an unfair advantage. There has always been a history of players dousing themselves with cooking oil or cooking spray. I am told Vaseline works just as well. Players want to prevent their opponent from being able to grab them. Some players will add stick-em to their gloves.

There are numerous ways that players may try to take some type of edge. They could try to prevent a player from grabbing them, or adjust the air pressure in a football so that it is more conducive to how they like to handle the ball. The League actually checks towels and gloves for illegal stick-um, as well as gauges the air pressure in game balls. Violations of League requirements may result in potential fines and game suspensions. I, as well as most players, try to excel with our performance within the rules of the game.

The League is always conscious of its image and actively protects it; while the media is just as active at trying to pick it apart. The big guy on the block is always being attacked; it's human nature. Envy fuels the desire to attack, and with the popularity of the League's controversies–whether real or perceived, it sells. Take the air pressure in game balls for example. Going back to the Super Bowl's of Troy Aikman and Brett Favre, the League would have a new football for every play. Game balls are highly sought after. A new ball is slippery and greasy and is a quarterback or receiver's nightmare.

Peyton Manning and Tom Brady worked with the League to address just what quarterbacks can do to season a ball to make it conducive during a game. The craziness of "Deflategate" lasted for a year...and will linger for years. Crazy? How much does it really affect the integrity of the competition and who is going to win?

To address these issues, the NFL changed the ball seasoning rules, stating that officials now must inspect the balls at halftime and following the final score of randomly selected games. Further, the footballs will be handled prior to every NFL game by:

- Wilson Sporting Goods will certify all pressure gauges prior to each season, providing every referee with one primary and one back up gauge. NFL Football Operations will have a supply as well, but the same gauge must be used for checking the PSI levels prior to, during or after a particular game.

- A member of NFL security will oversee to game officials recording the PSI levels of all twenty-four footballs prepared by each team (twelve primary and twelve backup) two hours and fifteen minutes before kickoff. Balls between 12.5 and 13.5 PSI will be approved, and balls outside of that range will be set to 13.0 PSI.

- Each ball will be numbered and stamped by the referee.

- A kicking ball coordinator, employed by the League, will assume custody of the balls until ten minutes before kick off, when he or she will be accompanied by a game official and a member of NFL security to the replay station. Security will then distribute twelve of the balls to each team's crew.

- At randomly selected games the balls will be checked at halftime by game officials and NFL security. At that point the twelve backup balls (stored in the officials' locker room) are escorted to the field. The air pressure will be checked at the end of randomly selected games.

- The referee is required to submit all pressure readings to the NFL by noon the following day.

Last-minute film review, discussions with coaches, and strategy discussions with other players take place just before heading out onto the field. I think every NFL team participates in a team prayer led by the head coach. Everyone takes a knee, holds hands and bows their heads. The head coach leads the team in prayer and generally the entire team recites "The Lord's Prayer." Generally, the procession onto the field is by position and the team heads out for the final preparation of warm ups as a team and before kickoff.

Chapter Eight

AWAY GAMES

Generally, when a team stays at a hotel, whether at training camp or for home or away games, the rules and policies are the same. Finances and logistics, rituals and habits take away distractions and surprises. The players are not allowed to order room service, nor are the players provided in-room mini-bars. We are not allowed to frequent the bar area; but, we do have access to staff-only gym areas, free Internet and perhaps movies.

Instead of room service and mini-bars, the hotel and the team provide protein-heavy menus for the players and coaches. Players and coaches generally pick from omelets, pancakes, French toast, hot and cold cereals, and snacks of fruit and ice cream. Snacks and lunches generally include burgers, wings and fajitas. Dinners allow for a lot of meat with beef, chicken, and fish, along with numerous types of vegetables and carbohydrates of potatoes, pastas and starches.

In the NFL, there are two pre-season and eight regular season away games. An NFL organization comprises between 150-200 people; this includes players, coaches and staff. Many of these people travel for away games. Well in advance, typically per season, there are accommodations made for approximately 200 rooms. There will be rooms for players, staff, coaches and family members. There is also consideration made for extra rooms if a player is sick and there is a need for isolation. The team will charter its own 777 or 747 airplane for all the players, coaches and staff, some media and fans.

Later in the day on a Friday before a Sunday game, before leaving the practice facility, the team provides each player with a team bag. This bag includes shower sandals, warm ups, soap, and a pre-game drink. The smaller pack bag is something that the player makes sure contains the incidentals that he personally desires for the road trip and is placed with the player's equipment. The players do not pack their own equipment. The team handles all of the logistics relating to the flight and hotel accommodations and the transportation of all the equipment that will be needed for the game.

The players are responsible for their own bag and whatever carry-on bag they want to bring with them of personal equipment and special pads. There are no baggage weight limits for the player. The team equipment staff has to be prepared for all sorts of weather. There is a lot of extra packaging for specialty equipment, extra helmets, shoulder pads, and shoes for all conditions, rain or snow, hot or cold.

Generally, about mid- morning, the players congregate at their training facility and board buses that will take them directly to the tarmac for their private TSA screening. All major airports have a private airport facility that allows for smaller jets as well as the 777 or 747 utilized by NFL teams. Just as with a commercial flight, the players are greeted by the flight crew and provided assistance by attendants. Coaches and veterans typically fly first class, while the progression back follows a similar hierarchy and order. Players on board are to conduct themselves in a manner that any passenger would who takes a long flight with family and friends.

The airline generally serves a meal. Players are either trying to get rest or are visiting with each other. Upon arrival at their destination, the players are shuttled on a team bus to the hotel. The hotel accommodations are similar to what has been previously described, as it is a goal for teams to provide structure and routine for the players. The mantra of finances and logistics in line with structure and discipline continues to play itself out with travel to away games. The least amount of surprises or deviations from a routine causes a minimization of distractions from a player's ability to focus and concentrate on the upcoming game.

Generally, the players are dressed in business attire and suits and ties. We are professionals in the most elite league in the world and want to present ourselves in the best fashion. There is the mind set that the attention to detail allows you to be focused on the upcoming game and to behaving, and performing as a professional. It is a tradition that most players recall from junior high through high school where you would wear ties on game day.

The pre-game arrival at the away stadium again follows, as much as possible, the routines that the players have put in place that were discussed for home games. While your home locker room is a home away from home, it is likely to be the cleanest and nicest environment that a player will encounter for a locker room. Generally, away stadium locker rooms are not as nice as your home locker room and are very dependent upon the age of the stadium involved. Some of the more recently built stadiums will have very nice locker rooms for the visiting team.

Very nice typically translates into a lot of space with large closet-style lockers, tile, and carpeting in the appropriate places. Regardless of when a game ends on the road, the flight home occurs shortly after the game. Generally, after the final whistle blows and a game is over, it takes around two hours from the end of the game to get to the tarmac to begin the flight home.

As fans tuck themselves into bed, or stay up late to watch a Sunday night game as they dread going to work Monday morning, we may not get back to the tarmac to fly back home until 1 or 2 a.m. Imagine the flight…there is a lot of snoring going on.

Upon arrival home, our team will shuttle us back to our facility where our cars are parked or players may have the ability to depart from the airport to their residence. It can be a mixture of whether or not players left vehicles at the airport, or traveled from the training facility on the shuttle to the tarmac. Again the team is quite accommodating in getting the players from point A to point B.

Game Time

The arena can be an experience that makes the hair rise on the back of your neck. Stadium mobs are controlled chaos. The twelfth man in Seattle registers on the Richter Scale. The last moments prior to the National Anthem, I draw upon what gives me my inspiration. As a veteran, I am able to tone out the hysteria in the arena and make it my normal.

I always have thoughts of my wife and children and my parents, but the immediate thought prior to taking my place before the National Anthem is to draw upon my inspiration; and that is my father. Jim Babin was an immigrant to this country from Canada. He was my first football coach and my mentor in life. He is always with me when I take the field.

Upon lining up for the National Anthem, I count my blessings for the country that we are in, and my love for our soldiers is deeply rooted to my core. I am always moved during the National Anthem and feel that we all should support our soldiers. I am committed to doing what I can to assist our soldiers in their responsibility of fulfilling their obligation and protecting our country's national defense.

I highly encourage others to do the same and recommend that notice is taken of the Servicemembers Civil Relief Act Foundation, Inc. What the foundation stands for is the focus of the book, *A Solider's Home: United States Servicemembers vs. Wall Street,* by my friend Matthew R. Cooper.

Upon taking the field and entering battle, a player must be aware that it is kill or be killed at all times. Team rules and NFL rules may linger in the back of your head, but you are playing to win the game. I am not concerned about the NFL rule relating to where my socks are on my calf.

If my team wants to fine me $575 for each pound that I may be over or under weight, that is up to their determination. Even though my Player's Union negotiated with the NFL that allows players to be fined in accordance with what the team weight requirements are, I am not now occupying my mind with such silliness.

As I take the field, I am identified by my number, 93. All players have a number on their jersey. There are players who will spend tens of thousands of dollars to acquire a number on a team. If the number you want is taken by a senior player then let the bidding begin. Bids from $10,000 to $100,000 could be the cost to a player wanting to obtain a particular number.

Generally, there is a meaning among what number you have; it could be related to a player's family, father, or astronomical sign. There are a 101 reasons a player may be drawn to a certain number. While a player may be drawn to a certain digit, there are of course rules relating to what number you may have in the NFL.

Rules, being rules, if there is not compliance, the result generally involves financial fines until a player is wearing the appropriate number. If a player does not wear a number commensurate with the rule covering his primary position, he will be fined until he gets a proper number.

1-9   Quarterbacks, Kickers and Punters (01-09 is never used)

10-19 Quarterbacks, Wide Receivers, Kickers and Punters

20-39 Running backs and defensive backs

40-49 Running backs, tight ends/half-backs, linebackers and defensive backs

50-59 Outside linebackers, defensive line and linebackers

60-79 Outside linebackers and defensive line

80-89 Wide Receivers and tight ends/halfbacks

90-99 Defensive line and linebackers

Significant to the number and position, it is most concerning whether a player is playing a position that allows him to be an eligible versus ineligible receiver. Therefore, players wearing numbers 50-79 must let a referee know that while they are playing in an eligible receiver position for that play, they are ineligible.

Numbers can mean a lot to a player. For example, Reggie Bush wanted to wear his number 5, just like he wore in college at USC. As that number is against the rules for a running back, he petitioned the NFL for a waiver. The NFL denied the request. Every year, there are numerous requests; so many requests such that if waivers were granted, the rules would not exist. Many players will actually wear their preferred number during mini-camps and practices, and follow NFL rules for the games.

Since college, I have always been 93. Each team I have played for, I have been able to acquire that number. Another perk of being a first-round draft pick and an all-around nice guy (or such a bad ass that I have been able to convince others that may have had an interest in 93) is that it would be best for me to have 93.

Prior to kick off, players may take notice of the fans. I am trying to make them my normal and tune them out so there is not a disruption in my focus, or an allowance for them to cause me to have an over-abundance of excitement. However, there are things that will draw our attention. I have noticed at times, that some fans will try to get the attention of a player by initiating contact in a very friendly and excited fashion.

Sometimes, the proximity causes the attempt at making friendly contact obvious. Upon an acknowledgment by the player to the fan, the fan will unfortunately display that it was merely a ploy by the fan to get the player's attention by acting as though it was a positive greeting. And when an acknowledgment by the player occurs, the fan gives the player a big "f*** you", and a tirade of horribly mean and degrading comments. This type of situation, I think, causes a lot of players to not allow their focus to be broken by what is happening in the stands.

It also is hard not to notice the fact that there is a cast of characters in the crowd. We do notice that. Many fans come dressed in completely outlandish and crazy costumes from a Jedi warrior to Santa Claus. There is a lot of fun and funny things happening in the stands. In some stadiums, it is quite common to see a fight break out among the fans. My noticing of the fans may occur a little during the pre-game. However, once the game starts, I do not notice them at all because I am in mortal combat.

During the pre-game, I will take notice of the weather conditions. Football is a unique sport in that it commences in times that it may be 100 degrees, and finish with temperatures well below zero, making it seem as if we played on frozen tundra. It is fascinating how at times you will see players in ten degree below zero weather wearing nothing but short-sleeved shirts. There are teams that make that a rule. There is a mind set that you are showing the other players that you do not care what the temperature is.

Weather does not affect you. You are coming into their house and weather is not an issue. You are all business. You are a gladiator. You are a warrior in mortal combat. You are not worried about the elements or something as silly as trying to stay warm. You are showing that you are concerned about what is at hand, and weather consideration is for losers or sissies.

I have noticed that there are many ways to deal with the elements without showing that it affects you. No matter what the conditions are, you need to have your body and metabolism functioning. Movement will keep you warm. In cold weather, many teams allow for a chicken soup broth on the sideline during the game. This obviously is not only a way of keeping you hydrated, but also allows for warmth. Cold weather can be conditioned.

Most tundra teams will practice in the elements. Your body does become conditioned to the colder weather. During the game, players may have heat packs within their gloves or in their shoes. There are temperature devices along the sidelines for keeping warm, as well as placing your helmet on to keep it warm. The equipment managers always prepare cold weather gear.

Along the sidelines, there is an extreme amount of technology. In cold weather, there will be the heated seats and helmet warmers. In warm weather, there may be fans or water hydration cooling machines. The NFL teams are equipped on the sidelines with the highest technology and communication devices to allow sideline coaches with headsets to speak with individuals in the coaches box high above the stadium or to a player on the field.

It is a requirement that both sides have equal access to the same type of technology. For example, if in cold weather the heat seats are off on one sideline, the other sideline has to turn theirs off. The important thing is that if the one sideline is able to get theirs working and the other has an awareness of it, they are allowed to turn theirs back on. Believe it or not, sometimes notice is not given that the heat seats are working again.

The equipment manager and team crews are among the best. They are highly trained professionals, committed to their professions. Interestingly, you will find multi-generations working in the equipment management and crew positions. It would be quite rare if there was ever a situation where something was needed–from replacement shoulder pads, knee pads to body girdles to odd parts to a helmet–that would not be readily accessible by the crew. Whatever a player needs is readily available by hardworking and dedicated crew members.

With all the brute force, speed, agility, and incredible strength being displayed on the field, it is nice knowing as an NFL football player that the medical care on our sidelines is the best. From the pre-game care that is provided to us by the best medical professionals available, it is nice knowing that we have physicians specializing in orthopedic surgery and sports medicine on our sidelines, and are fully prepared to provide us with the care necessary in the event of an injury.

NFL Medical

Recently, there is a new policy in the NFL, that the team head doctor for each team has to introduce themselves to the head referee. Before the game, the medical personnel become familiar with the referees so that in the event of an injury, there is no question as to who is needed. There are around thirty medical professionals staffing each NFL game.

There are independent athletic trainers, ophthalmologists, dentists, radiology technicians, airway management physicians, EMTs, paramedics, orthopedist, primary care physicians, chiropractors, and neurotrauma consultants. The emergency airway management physicians are typically anesthesiologists or emergency medicine physicians. Typically, the emergency airway management physicians wear a red hat and stand between the 30 to 40-yard line.

The NFL mandates that all stadiums have X-ray machines on site to diagnose fractures or dislocations. Essentially, the sidelines and the locker room are small emergency rooms. What becomes very interesting in the NFL is that with all of this expert medical care available, there is the dichotomy between when a player will utilize the medical professionals versus playing through an injury and not letting the team/trainers/MDs become aware of your conditions and pain. Keep in mind, the players are trying to earn a living and stay in the League of their dreams.

A veteran obviously has more ability than a rookie or first-round draft pick in working with a club concerning his injuries. These differences center around the investment a team has in a player and the contract that may exist. In the case of a first-round draft pick, they always have an upper hand via the credibility of a team's scouting department at stake. Teams expend a lot of money on scouting and justify the expenditure by standing by their first round tags.

It is quite different for rookies, regardless of their draft selection. There is an old expression, "You don't make the club in the tub." Everything a rookie does is tracked. You do not want people reading too much into what you may report to a trainer. As an example, consider all of the attention that is now being given to concussions. There are those who argue about the different levels and whether it is even an injury to the brain.

Who has the training and experience necessary to be able to properly diagnose a concussion? Are there objective tests that are used? Is medical evidence utilized? Is it a knee-jerk reaction to all of the media attention and hoopla surrounding the condition that the label/diagnosis is quickly handed out?

I see guys every day in camp puking and enduring achy heads and fighting feelings of dizziness; not because they suffered a concussion, but because it is over 90 degrees and they have been working their butts off for hours and are exhausted. Could some knucklehead diagnose you with a concussion because you have been playing football for a couple hours because your head hurts, you are dizzy, and puking?

At the other end of the spectrum, obviously where there is a traumatic injury, it is wonderful to know that there are the necessary medical professionals to give you the treatment you will need commensurate with the injury; from the sideline to hospitalization in any of the finest care facilities in our country.

NFL Referees

The refs in the NFL are among the best. The vast majority of the NFL officials are business owners, or hold senior management positions of large corporations. For most, being an NFL official is a second career. As NFL referees earn between $75,000 and $200,000 per year, many attempt to make the referee position a full-time job. The NFL transports referees first class to the games that they will referee that weekend, and also cover all of their expenses. Being a referee takes between twenty-five to thirty hours a week.

Therefore, as a second job, you can see that they have quite a taxing schedule. From Friday to Monday, they are consumed with their NFL positions. A former referee grades each official in every game.

They are under a tremendous amount of pressure and are held to the highest standards of accountability. Every action and call is observed from the eye in the sky. They go through many game reviews and critiques.

Players try to give the referees respect...they better. No touching or yelling as it will bring stiff fines and possible ejection from the game. I try to play the game as though they are not there. I cannot allow human fallibility that is authoritative and unchallengeable effect my performance. I am too busy doing my job and leave the refs alone and trust them to do their job. I try to leave it all out on the field and play with the most mayhem and violence as I possibly can.

I like to do my playing with violence, sacks, tackles, forced fumbles and wins. It is quite common to have many different types of trash-talking players on the field. Players will try to do whatever they can to get an edge. Some believe that getting into your head will have an effect on your performance. Generally, players try to be professional with one another.

However, tempers can flare and tirades can occur both verbally and physically. Every name imaginable and aspersion known has been thrown around a football field. Many players do not talk trash. They try to focus on their tasks at hand. Many simply learn that they are not trash-talkers, simply because they are not good at it. Trash talkers try to come up with something that they think will rile up the opposing player across from them.

Sometimes their jibber jabber will back fire. While they are trying to get into your head, there will be a lapse in their ability to focus that may give you the upper hand. You hear a lot of players talk about other guys' wives, girlfriends and mothers. That seems to be a common theme in trying to push your opponents buttons. Trash talking on a field of play is quite distinguishable from the recent discussions of political correctness relating to bullying.

Trash talking is directed at an opponent wherein the type of language used with a teammate would fall into the category of bullying. Talking trash in your locker room with fellow teammates obviously is destructive and is something that should not be tolerated. Sometimes there becomes a fuzzy line between trash talking, bullying and simply engaging in "boys will be boys" good-natured ribbing. Even in the field of play, ribbing your teammates or opposing players can be all part of the fun of playing the game. All of it is taking place in the NFL during a game and in our locker rooms.

Trash talking among some, is taking the fun and putting forth the effort as a means of attempting to gain an edge. Some players may use it as a means to hype themselves up, or attempt to intimidate the player on the other side of the ball. During a game, guys are doing whatever they can to get your goat. After a play, perhaps they step on your toe while they are walking back to the huddle or make a comment about your wife.

Example: I am trying to sack the quarterback and the guy across from me is trying to prevent me from running and getting a tackle. Over the course of the season or years in the NFL, we may face each other on many occasions. While there are many players that form a respect for one another, this is a very serious business and defensive players want tackles and sacks. If I have an offensive player take cheap shots physically or verbally in an attempt to confuse and rile me up, I have to either allow myself not to be taken in and break my focus, or get the better of him in all levels of competition.

We know who the other players are. We know where they came from and where they spend the off-season. I am smart enough to study their behavior on the field through hours of film. If there is information that I become aware of (such as their home town or where they like to vacation or spend the off season) I always like to add a personal touch to what I may say. This will cause them to wonder how I know where they live and that I will be seeing them in the back waters of Louisiana the next time they go fishing.

If anything, for that moment, they are caused to contemplate and think of anything other than their field of play action, and I have just gained the upper hand. Guys who love cars are easily thrown into a break in their concentration if you start talking about how their Mustang or Impala is child's play and does not stand a chance against my Barracuda. It is easy to get into the heads of a motor head.

The only way that I have learned to silence a trash-talker is to not engage him verbally. If my blocker is spouting off and I get a sack, that is the best way to shut him up. A team win always clinches the deal. The opposing forces that play in the situation are the players that think that trash-talking is a source of humor and entertainment, whereas the NFL feels that it is disrespectful to the game. When there is a fight during the game, it can generally be traced back to a cheap shot that resulted from the volatility of the game or is a product of frustration or the flaring of tempers due to trash talk.

The NFL, seeking to curb trash talking and eliminate it, is a result of the fact that it many times, is the root of a fight or bench-clearing brawl. It has tried to crack down on trash talking and has made rules that specifically prohibit it. There is quite a distinction among fights during an NFL game, which are rare, than those fights that occur at camp on the practice field. When there are ninety men fighting for a slot on a fifty-three-man roster, there is much frustration and tempers flare. Temperatures are hot and players are exhausted. Training camp fights are more akin to a scuffle that is quickly broken up.

Fights during a game are strictly prohibited and rarely occur. Helmets are quite hard. Punching one is more likely to do damage to the hand than to the person receiving the blow. Compared to baseball, hockey or even basketball, the fights among NFL games are rare, given that the nature of the game itself allows the player to exercise aggression or hostilities they feel compelled to express during the play of action. There is no need to exert violence after the whistle blows given that during the play whatever act of violence that wants to be perpetrated is typically allowed.

The trash talking that occurs among players sometimes occurs as a result of the competitiveness among players that regularly see each other. Within the division, we play some of our strongest rivalries. These rivalries occur as a result of trying to beat the other team out of getting to the playoffs, as well as just the competitiveness of playing against the same player on a regular basis.

Generally, rivalries can be categorized as a team versus team; players versus players; or, players versus positions. The players do feel the rivalries among team versus team in that we are trying to beat the other team to get into the playoffs. In the same fashion, you will see the rivalry between offensive versus defensive players. NFL Players are very competitive. When we are facing an opponent on a regular basis, we want to be the one that dominates each play as players and ultimately have your team win.

In addition, there will be a rivalry between different positions. As a defensive end, I want to sack the quarterback and obviously the quarterback is doing everything he can to avoid that. This can get carried to extremes when you see defensive players hating certain offensive positions, and generally that is directed toward quarterbacks. If you are not allowed to touch them, how are you supposed to sack them? Some of the funniest media commentators, center around how much defensive players hate quarterbacks. Aside from the fact that you cannot hit them, the astronomical pay they receive only fuels the defenders fire on trying to get to them in time before they release the ball.

Fights are generally broken down into scuffles that occur between teammates at camp or all out bench-clearing brawls. There is the extreme rarity of teammates locking horns in the locker room. There are also fights that are conducted through the media, and the continued verbal assaults that fly through Twitter and Instagram. The most common thread among all of these conflicts is the extreme competitiveness of the League. Players are fighting to stay in the NFL, and that can lead to a very emotional situation concerning one's temper while using all of their physical attributes to impose extreme physical violence and harm to their opponent.

On the sidelines, the players are generally focused on what is happening in the game. Players play to win. Nevertheless, the NFL has passed rules specifically designed to apply to the bench area and its borders, and have attempted to regulate the permitted sideline movements of the players during a game. The NFL cites safety purposes as reasoning for regulating members of the chain-gang, coaches, players and other club personnel in the bench areas.

The NFL has made it a requirement that each team appoint a "get-back" coach. The sidelines can be described as a place where there is a fun and exciting gathering with complete and utter chaos. It is fun and exciting or complete and utter chaos depending upon who's perspective you are viewing the situation. From a coach's perspective, it is chaos.

There are offensive guys visiting with the defensive group, there are young guys running all over the place, veterans are no where to be found, there is the get-back coach trying to hold back a torrential flood with a teaspoon. Players are constantly pushing and shoving and are always trying to get as close to the sideline as possible. There is a constant chaos and crowding of the officials and concern for their safety has resulted in the sideline rules by the NFL.

For a coach concerned about team performance, sideline organization is critical. There is a section for offensive players and defensive players and the need for coordination within those groups. Substitutions are constantly being made and the need for order and trying to call plays. In addition, there is a constant need to try to organize where the players are on the sidelines between offensive, defensive, special teams, etc.

At best, you are trying to achieve organized chaos. If the chaos becomes so much that the chain gang is interrupted or has the potential of impacting on the field of play near the sidelines, there could be in-game penalties and other disciplinary actions taken. There are rules for game operations. Believe it or not, there are policy manuals issued by the NFL for the teams that include rules relating to the borders that are restrictive of the movement of personnel.
Throughout the manual, including the sideline rules, the NFL has voluminous manuals and rulebooks, which spell out all rules and regulations as though they came from a law library.

No law library can regulate what our friends, Larry, Moe and Curly are doing in a scrum. Imagine the diction in a legal treatise addressing or trying to prohibit Larry from doing an oil- check on Moe, or Curly executing a fish-hook on Larry, while Moe draws forward an eye-gouge or a spit in the face. What is a scrum you may ask, or an oil-check or a fish-hook?

Chapter Nine

NFL UNOFFICIAL LINGO

Bust – A draft pick, generally the high draft pick that does not play to expectations.

CBA – Collective Bargaining Agreement – a contract between players and the owners. The deal is generally around $12 to $16 billion dollars a year. The NFL is so huge that the generalization of $16 billion simply allows 4 billion dollars to float. I do not have a calculator and I am not coming up with this figure through calculations, but to have the generalization in the billions is incredible. The NFL even has its own television network.

Cheat Week – this is the week that players that are extremely focused on their diet and nutrition allow for a week of eating everything that they do not allow themselves to eat the rest of the year such as: Doritios, hot fudge sundaes, chili cheese dogs, cheeseburgers, etc.

Check Down – a short pass to the nearest player. Generally a running back or tight end, when the primary receiver is not open.

Chop Block – an illegal block where an offensive player drops down and hits the opposing player below the knees. It is a dangerous play that can result in the ending of a career due to injuries.

Chucking – a lineman causes a contact by extending his arms against typically the offensive player trying to block him and followed by a quick reaction with an intent to create space between the players to then move around the other player.

Clip – an illegal block generally across the back.

Clock It – when the quarterback throws the ball immediately to the ground after receiving it from center to stop the clock. The clock stops because the quarterback's action is an incomplete pass.

Digits –numbers that players want to wear and are allowed to wear.

Directives – NFL or team recommendations to players or binding rules relating to everything from media contact, to sex and sleep.

Exotics – the flea-flickers or gadget plays.

Eye-Gouge – the act of inserting one's stiffened finger into the eye-ball of an opposing player in an attempt to divert his focus from an attempt to recover a fumbled football.

Finger Bang a/k/a Oil Check – the act of an opposing player taking sometimes two, or generally a formation of three of his fingers and with great force, attempting to insert the fingers in the opposing player's anus. This action is taken with the thought that it would cause a distraction upon the recipient to loosen their grip or end their effort to recover a football.

Fish-Hook – a very dangerous tactic taken as it involves injecting one's finger into the mouth of another with the hope of not allowing the finger to be engaged within the recipient's teeth. The purpose of which is inflict great pain, pulling the cheek outwardly from the rest of the recipient's face in an effort to get the recipient to cease their efforts in obtaining a fumbled football. Generally preferred by the recipient not to have occurred after the injected finger had been previously involved in an oil-check.

Flea-Flicker – a trick play. One of the coolest in history is the globe of death where the kick receivers huddle with all the players in tight and pass the ball to a specific player but then all of the players take off in different directions as if they have the ball and no one really knows who has the ball. The more common flea flicker is where a receiver is on a stop route and they catch the ball and pitch it to another player sprinting past them that is not covered by a defender.

Gadget Play – similar to a flea-flicker such as a double reverse pass.

Grey Beards – Players from the 60's, 70's and 80's. These players always think that they had the toughest time in the NFL because they were not getting paid that much and they had double-day practices during camp and it was always an all-out brutal practice where you beat the heck out of each other; and they are probably rightfully so wearing such with a badge of honor.

Grid Iron – a frame of parallel bars. The football field is marked with a grid of parallel lines and is therefore referred to as a grid iron.

Gunner – on a kick, generally a punt, the fastest player that is running down to try and tackle the person catching the ball.

Hail Mary – a very long pass made in desperation as a last ditch effort with the smallest chances ever of success.

Hot Read – immediately after the quarterback gets the ball from center, then throws to a receiver as a result of the quarterback's belief that the defense is about to blitz. The quarterback makes this decision as he approaches the initiation of the play.

Huddle – the offensive and defensive players prior to a play forming together in a group to call a play in secret so that the opposing team cannot hear the play being called. Generally a huddle is broken with all of the players clapping their hands. This is a custom that goes back in time in trying to have the players play in unison with one another. They are part of a team and are going forward to execute the play as a team and it starts through the comradeship of breaking the huddle.

Injury Time Out – when the clock stops so that a team can help an injured player diagnose and treat a condition that they just received in the field of play. Most of the time it is for a legitimate reason, but sometimes it is fairly obvious given the circumstances that a player may be faking an injury in an effort to stop the clock at an opportune time.

Instant Replay – an attempt by the officials to review what just occurred on the playing field. Generally, even after an instant replay is reviewed for 5, 10 or 15 minutes, there is still room for argument.

Jelly-Belly – must be jelly because jam don't shake like that. Not the type of player like Mike Golic eating donuts before a game. All players in the NFL are elite athletes despite what some may feel their appearances may portray. Some guys in the NFL might eat 10,000 calories a day and you will not find an ounce of fat on them. Some eat science diets and strict rules of nutrition and some are on seefood diets – they see food and they eat it.

Juke a/k/a Ankle-Breaker – the speed, agility and quickness of a player to move around another while the other's mind is trying to figure out what direction a player is going and cannot direct the body to move in conjunction with their mental efforts.

Line Dance – not an uptown funk type of move; but dancing around 350 pounders to break through to get the quarterback or ball carrier.

Living In a Bubble – the concept that as a player you are in a partnership with your team and you should take care of yourself physically, emotionally and legally. Do not play with fireworks or go running with the bulls or swimming with the sharks or not being honest with the medical staff, or behave in a manner that will get you arrested. An NFL player is living in a bubble and should professionally manage their end of their partnership with their team and the NFL.

Mooch – the guy that is always forgetting the food or snacks that he wants and is eating off your plate.

NFL – Not For Long, or the National Football League, which is the League containing the American and National Football Conferences, see CBA $$$, NFL television network, etc., etc., billions and billions of dollars.

NFLPA – The NFL Player's Association. This is the labor organization of the players, which was founded in 1956.

Neutral Zone – the space between the offensive and defensive lines of scrimmage. No player may stand within this zone prior to the ball being snapped.

Nickel Defense – this is usually employed in obvious passing situations with a defensive alignment using five defensive backs.

OTA – Organized Team Activity. OTAs are anything organized by the team for its players from mini-camps to recreational activities from a spa day to a movie to a bowling tournament.

Pancake – When a player knocks another player on his back and plants his backside to the turf.

Paria – a person that is despised or avoided and generally considered low class.

PAT – Point After Touchdown. A touchdown is six points. After a touchdown a team can choose to kick for an extra one point or trying to score a two point conversion. At one time, the ball was put on the second yard line for the kick; in the 2015 season it was moved to the fifteen yard line.

    The two point conversion is still on the second yard line. The rule change did not make sense. It was an attempt to spice up the game; but, was counter-intuitive regarding player safety, and puts too much importance on what the one point was meant to be.

Play Clock – the length of a game is sixty minutes, divided into four quarters of fifteen minutes each. Half time is twelve minutes. The time between plays from the end of a given play to the snap of a ball is forty seconds; after a certain administrative stopping or game delays, that time is twenty-five seconds.

Pistol – an offensive formation that is a take off from the shotgun and spread formation. The quarterback is three to four yards back from the center as opposed to a shotgun where the quarterback is 5-7 yards.

    In a pistol, the running back is with the quarterback. The

Pistol allows the quarterback a better view of the defense and he can either hand to the running back or still pass.

Pooch Kick – it is a hard, line driven shot of a kick designed to bounce off the opposing players so that the receiving team may recover the ball as it is bouncing around.

Prima Donna - a person with an inflated opinion of their talent.

Run and Shoot – a designed play where the quarterback may run the ball or throw it. It is generally a type of offense the team runs in that the receivers and running backs are spread out, which causes the defense to not know whether it will be a running play or a pass play.

Sack – when a defensive player is able to tackle the quarterback before he is able to pass the ball and tackle him behind the line of scrimmage. The NFL first recorded this action as a "sack" in 1961. The term prior to that was the "dump"; used when the defensive player was able to "dump" the "passer".

Historically, the term "sack" has been credited to Hall of Famer Deacon Jones, who described the act of "sacking" a quarterback before he could pass the ball. Former NFL coach Marv Levy believed it was Washington Redskins' coach George Allen who started the term. Allen used it when the Redskins played their rivals, the Dallas Cowboys. Allen said (about what the Redskins would do to Craig Morton of the Cowboys) that the Cowboys were "going to take that Morton Salt and pour him into a sack".

Scrum – the pile-up and fight for a fumble recovery.

Shotgun – an offensive formation where the quarterback lines up 5-7 yards behind the center. When the center snaps the ball, the quarterback is already in position to throw a pass.

Spit in Face – taking liquid from one's mouth and projecting it into the face of an opposing player to infuriate them to the extent that their attention is diverted from recovering a fumbled football.

Stooge – once popularized by the stooges, Larry, Moe, Curly and Shemp, but more authoritatively understood as a person who plays a subordinate role to a principal, or an unimportant person controlled by a powerful organization, or a performer who is able to live his dreams and make those who feel they are in command look foolish.

Stunt – defensive players working in unison to disrupt the offensive play and hopefully leading to a sack or a tackle for loss of yardage.

Super-Sonic Atomic Wedgie – back before players were paid millions of dollars, something that would commonly occur during the hazing of a rookie.

Sudden Death – In overtime when the next score determines who wins the game.

Super Bowl – the Championship game between the AFL and NFL. On January 15, 1967 Super Bowl I was played and the Green Bay Packers beat the Kansas City Chiefs 35-10. It is said that Lamar Hunt, former owner of the Kansas City Chiefs, came up with the name. A popular new toy at the time was the "super ball". It was a bowl game, a championship game, a super bowl. Hunt added roman numerals (similar to world wars) given the importance and seriousness of each game. In 2015, every football field had the 50-yard line marked with gold numerals. The 2015 season Super Bowl (played in 2016) was Super Bowl 50.

Trash Talker – takes many forms from the jokester on your team ribbing fellow teammates to opponents trying to get into your head.

Tuck Rule – a fumble to an incomplete pass. What was a fiction in the NFL from 2001-2013. The tuck rule took a fumble and made it an incomplete pass.

Wedge-Buster – Not the guy that polices the anti-atomic wedgie, but the actual lead person on the kick-off team that breaks up the blocking scheme set forth by the receiving team.

Chapter Ten

THE FINAL WHISTLE BLOWS

"It ain't over until it is over." This is a statement that rings most true in its use describing the final moments of a football game. Games literally come down to the final second. Typically there is back and forth action. Many games, at first, appear as blowouts with true come back stories that if told as fiction, would not be believed.

Busted–mentally and physically drained. Immediately after a game, there are thoughts about getting ready for next week. The thoughts automatically flash through your mind. It becomes a matter of routine where your head is always getting ready for the game next week. Celebrations are short and meaningless given the goals and objectives in mind.

Immediately after a game, many players walk around the field, while some quietly slip into the locker room. This is the time that players may spend with friends from the other team. It is also the time when those who are interested in collecting memorabilia will take this as an opportunity to make swaps. After a game, there is a large group of players and coaches from both teams, as well as some officials, who meet together in prayer.

They meet somewhere on the field before heading into the locker rooms. On the field, there may be some players providing post-game interviews depending on their contractual requirements for coaches and players to meet with the media.

The sudden end to the intensity and flow of adrenalin, coupled with having worked your body-muscles and joints to exhaustion, has an interesting affect on your mind and body...not to mention the pain. There is a lot of pain, swelling, bruising and stiffness. The body is a machine. It requires fuel and lubricants. There is an immediate need to replenish your body with hydration and proteins. Throughout the game we are pumping the fluids; Gatorade and water. Our muscles are warn out and are breaking down.

Physiologically, our "storage facilities" have been depleted and our protein reserves will be tapped into. Our protein reserves are our muscles. We cannot afford that breakdown. We need food now!

Immediately awaiting players in a post-game locker room is a large supply of food. Finances and logistics. It's usually something quick and easy to devour by filthy and hungry players. Typically this is pizza or sub sandwiches. While eating and hydrating, your mind cannot help but reflect upon your game performance. Stellar performance and mistakes dominate your mind's eye as it replays specific events.

Tomorrow morning's film sessions cannot come soon enough for the good plays, but may come too quickly for the bad and ugly performance reviews. An NFL field has film coverage from every conceivable angle. Your performance is everything. Nothing is guaranteed in the NFL. Monday film can bring accolades or the directive of turning in your playbook.

This is a game? Right? It is the most cutthroat business that could possibly exist. There are approximately 1,695 players in the NFL holding positions that millions of world-class athletes hunger for, and would give their left nut for the opportunity to play. While you are trying to replenish your body, all of this is racing through your head. You are physically and mentally exhausted and have a million and one thoughts racing through your head, not to mention you have yet to get out of your uniform.

The several sizes too small jersey is now a sweaty, greasy, slimy, stinky article that is seemingly permanently attached to your body. The process of peeling (and what seems like tearing) it away requires the help from several others. Careful though, stitching and numbers require care because remember, you only get two home and two away jerseys for the season. Teams are great at getting the mess off of you and all clean and pressed for the next game.

To top it off, locker rooms are a breeding ground for germs. Therefore, the staff is quick to gather up the filthy uniforms and put the locker room back in order as we eat and cleanse. Saying that a locker room is a breeding ground for germs is putting it lightly and kindly. There have been instances where teams have had MRSA (Methicillin Resistant Staphylococcus Aureus) concerns in their locker room. A deadly staph infection is not taken lightly. Benches, lockers (our closets) and our personal chairs must always be clean and maintained in pristine fashion. Not because we are Prima Donnas; but, so we do not get infections that have threatened some with the potential for loss of limb.

Hydration, food and air. Generally, the locker rooms are equipped with high-tech ventilation systems. We need fuel and lubricants. High horse-powered muscle cars need fuel, lubricants and cannot have combustion without oxygen. Similarly, we need the hydration, protein and fuel for our blood cells. It is all about taking care of your people from the team's prospective. It is all geared toward our health and safety. The beast is being paid handsomely... feed the beast...take care of the beast. The teams in the NFL take care of the beast, their investment, very well.

Most locker rooms are very nice. As mentioned before, we have large closets as our locker, with plenty of cubbies, shelving, and the ability to hang our clothing freely. Our home lockers generally have a cubby that has an electronic locking device. On away games, we are given a bank bag that corresponds with our number. We place our valuables in there, which is retained by equipment staff. The NFL locker room is quite a secure place. I am not aware of any instances of theft.

After stripping and eating (or eating and stripping), you now have a desire to shower. All of this takes place among numerous members of the media. There are approximately sixty players and coaches who need to shower. If it is an away game and at an older stadium, there may only be fifteen shower heads, which work at most with a mere dribble. The best are nicely tiled and mirrored country-club style locker rooms with about thirty shower heads. Given the wide variety of activities of what players are doing after a game, the flow of players getting their turn at a shower generally occurs quite orderly.

Showers can feel great or cause more pain. Turf burn with water applied is a mean, painful experience. Coming in out of the cold, where you feel at times that your skin has been frozen and then torn from your body only has the pain exacerbated in the shower. Most of the time, it feels great to get clean and feel your muscles coming back to life.

To meet the away game time crunch from whistle to tarmac in two hours, there is not enough time. Things are a rush. Keep in mind, during this time as well, many players have members of the media waiting at their locker, and some, after getting cleaned up, attend an organized press conference. Notice the difference between a half-naked player after a game standing for an interview at his locker, compared to a cleaned up version at a post-game press conference.

Pay particular attention to a player's eyes. Exhaustion is easy to read and see. Sometimes it is mistaken for anger, sadness or frustration; but, it is pure exhaustion. Mentally and physically, all of what you have was left on the field. Physically, your body is suffering and the player has not yet had the opportunity to replenish. Hydration and nutrition is not just a good idea and deserved, but what is needed to allow our body to keep functioning normally.

At post-game press conferences after the showers, a player's body has been allowed to re- hydrate, consume protein and stop its stores from robbing/breaking down its reserves. You will see a completely different player after hydration; just look into the eyes. When guys retire from the NFL, what you hear most of the time is how much they miss the camaraderie, the brotherhood of having someone else's back and knowing they have yours. They miss the locker room.

After a game is over the camaraderie is no different than practice as it relates to the fun and antics you see in the locker room. It is a fun experience. You have a whole cast of characters: warriors, gladiators, jokesters, officers and gentlemen. These are not guys living in a bubble. They are the sort that run with the bulls, swim with the sharks, walk along biplanes, or the types who mess around with a lot of different women…and those that are good husbands and fathers. It is quite a variety of different types of guys. It really provides for a dynamic and interesting situation.

It generally is quite a collegiate, fun atmosphere. I have drawn distinctions between fighting during training camp and fighting during a game; rarely does it occur in the locker room. Players own the locker room. It is their locker room. The players need to have control over their locker room.

While there are situations (as the one that occurred in 1976 between Roger Staubach and Clint Longley, or in August of 2015 with Geno Smith), given the number of guys and the years and years that have gone through the locker room, I would speculate that the positive interactions and the solidifying of player relationships; the positive far outweighs the negative conflicts. Fighting in a locker room is purely destructive to a team's dynamics.

As mentioned earlier, it can be a fun, hysterical atmosphere. However, there is an obvious fine line that sometimes becomes cloudy and is difficult to discern whether there is inappropriate behavior from one player toward another. Hazing is closely regulated. Whether or not there could be a Richie Incognito type situation playing out is always of great concern. Incognito was quite a gregarious individual and some (Goodell) say it was difficult to determine boundaries and inappropriate versus appropriate behavior.

Most of the time, the players are like family and are really trying to just have a good time. It is important though that a good time is not had at another's expense. The dynamics, I imagine, are like any other work place whether you have a law firm or a small construction crew. Are people getting along or being entertained at another's expense? I guess bullying is a human behavior that always has to be monitored, regardless of where it happens; from preschool to a NFL locker room.

After a home game, players are free to leave whenever they desire. Hopefully, a player has family or friends waiting for him. Every player receives two home game tickets and there is a lot of trading going on among the players depending upon their need or lack thereof, and there is also easy access to purchase more tickets.

What an NFL player does after leaving the stadium is as broad and wide of a spectrum as what other people do when they get out of work. Most of the time, most of us are rather tired and want to go home and spend time with our family and friends. If it is a late game, we obviously want to go home and sleep. I usually drive my car from the hotel so that I can drive directly home from the stadium. The team is very good about whether a player needs to have access to a shuttle to the hotel to get their vehicle or whatever their needs may be.

After getting home from a home game, I continue with the hydration and eat large amounts of lean protein. I enjoy eating venison or elk. If it is an away game, the food that is available in the locker room is again something that is quick and easy. However, when we get on the plane, there is a wide variety of very good food with lean meats and vegetables and other sources of protein and carbohydrates. There is a constant focus on proactive health. Hydration, food and sleep are the focus of away games and the return home. I like to stay on top of injuries, whether turf burns or bruising. Being proactive with these types of injuries prohibit them from becoming more serious and allows you to get ready for the next game.

Most players spend a quiet evening at home re-hydrating, consuming proteins, and introducing large quantities of ice to various parts of their body just trying to recover. Generally, Monday is a light day physically, and Tuesday, according to our CBA, is a day off. By Wednesday, your body needs to be rejuvenated and ready to go.

With all that being said, playing in a game in the NFL is probably one of the most fun and exhilarating experiences I will have in my life. From the moment I get out of bed to head toward the hotel for a home game, or the tarmac for an away game, to when my head is on my pillow at home once again, everything in between is one of the most incredible experiences one can have.

Chapter
Eleven

ROUTINE & DISCIPLINE
The Weekly Schedule

Playing in the NFL is glorious and provides someone with the opportunity to live out the dream. The price paid is tremendous sacrifice, pain and physical and mental discipline. These are the essentials for enduring the physicality of the game. Nutrition, diet and physical health and proactive medical care all allow for the proper soothing of muscle and musculature development. Cold soaks and massages are necessary to prevent a bruise or aliment from becoming serious.

For years, I have slept in a hyperbaric chamber. Take a look at what a hyperbaric chamber is. You will immediately take note that it takes great mental fortitude to have a good night's sleep in your own personal coffin-like apparatus. The evening after a game involves a lot of ice. The immediate morning after a game, the soreness and stiffness sets in, and the pain increases.

Pain is the body's signal that something is amiss. Beyond the alarm of trying to sooth and resolve the aliments, there is the enduring of the feeling itself. Cold soaks and massages, combined with intermittent applications of cold to heat to cold to heat, and proper diet and nutrition, are the best proactive manners of reconciliation.

The current NFL schedule is four pre-season games and sixteen regular season games, including a biweekly game. This is a bare minimum without the playoffs, Super Bowl or Pro Bowl games. A player is looking at approximately twenty-one weeks per season. Beyond the physical sacrifice and demands, there are times where a player may reside under the same roof during this time period as his family, or he may be away in another part of the country. Living away from your wife and kids demands incredible sacrifice and putting oneself in the proper frame of mind.

The NFL is fun and rewarding in many respects. There are around 1,600 players with millions of people wanting their jobs. The financial reality of life, balanced with quality time with family, is a difficult proposition. Most players love playing in the NFL. There is nothing that they could be doing that would be better than that experience. A player, after their NFL career is over, will not feel that he has any complaints or regrets about having gone down that path. There are great opportunities and rewards for the player's entire family and the player develops close friendships that will last a lifetime. The bonding among NFL players is among the strongest bonds of friendship.

MONDAY

The schedule for the Monday following a Sunday game has a lot to do with whether or not the game the day before was won or lost. Many times, if the team wins, the following Monday means there is an off day. However, an off day in the NFL never really means that it is a day off. Players are playing for the physicality of the game, the challenge, the fun, and the desire to determine what it is they are able to endure.

A day off simply means there is less organized team activity and less structure provided by the team and it's coaches. Regardless of whether the game the day before was a victory or a loss, Monday is the most important day of the week because it allows the player to be proactive in their desire to maintain top physical health. Win or lose, generally a player will go to the practice facility to watch film, do cold soaks and have muscle massages.

Monday is also the first weight lifting session of a new week. While a weight lifting program may vary between the off-season, pre-season, and the actual season, a player is always lifting weights and working out to maintain their strength and conditioning.

My workout schedule, while it is my trade secret, is generally broken down between the weight-room versus my overall workout, depending on the season. I do love working out and lifting weights. I am particularly fond of core activities, such as chin-ups, pull-ups and dips. One of the most difficult feats of strength that I challenge people to do, is a good work out on the dip rack. Try doing three sets of twenty-five on a dip rack, or strap 50-100 lbs. to your waist and do a number of dips.

I realize that most men going through their daily lives cannot do more than one or two dips without feeling as though they are going to split their chest apart. It is a testosterone high to grab a couple of 150-pound dumbbells and press them off the bench. Our bodies are machines. Developing musculature, quite simply put, feels great.

Playing on the football field requires more than just speed and quickness. Strength, power and explosiveness can only be accomplished through the development of the proper muscle groups. I believe in an overall development through workouts with weights and core building exercises. Workouts involving dips, chin-ups, pull-ups, sit-ups and push-ups can be the most grueling.

An NFL player's goal is to build strength and power while maintaining flexibility. The off-season is generally where the player builds and maximizes his muscle growth and development. During the season you still have to build muscle, maintain it, and stay highly flexible and in good condition. Even though I may be in pain and sore on Monday, I still kick the week off with a good workout.

The training goals focus on overall strength and endurance. I build muscle for power and speed. I need explosiveness off the ball and upper body strength to support the leverage I drive from my lower body powerhouse. Everything centers on the core; one's guttural constitution. Football takes guts, both mental and physical. Physically, a football player needs guts to endure the strength, speed, endurance demands, and pain management. To accomplish this, working out is a way of life for me. I am in training twelve months a year.

Wherever I am living at the time or visiting, I have easy access to the implements necessary for me to get a workout. My home and ranch have what I need on site. If I am visiting an exotic location, or in Paw Paw, Michigan visiting my Uncle Phil and Aunt Mary, I am able to find a way to stay with my training no matter where I am.

I love building my powerhouse like Walter Payton loved running the hills. There is nothing better than running the hills to the point beyond pain, and developing explosiveness by sprinting with a mini-parachute. One of my favorite things to do at the ranch is to run sprints while pulling my wife and kids on our 1,000-pound ATV. Building your core requires the most difficult tasks. It is hard to do for a reason.

The old clichés of "no pain, no gain", or "anything worthwhile takes a lot of effort", are true. Add seventy-five pounds around your waste doing dips or running sprints with a quad strapped to your shoulders. Flipping tractor tires, chopping wood and chasing fallow deer, all help tear up your guts…and is fun and interesting.

I include more traditional methods as well, like free weights and machines. Bench press, squats, dead lifts, curls, dumbbells, flies, pull-ups and pull-downs; if there is an exercise or a particular form, I have tried it or do it regularly. Physical exercise and conditioning is fun and entertaining for the entire family. Hiking and climbing, lifting weights and running around the ranch, beats eating chips and lying on the couch watching TV.

A family that does crunches together enjoys everything and anything together. The Babins do not lie on the beach when we go on vacation. We tear it up with sprints and exciting games of catch. The Kennedy's enjoyed rambunctious games of touch football after their Thanksgiving dinner. The Babins get down and dirty and come out of the back yard drenched in sweat.

I like to work my muscle groups with a day of rest. I work out every day. Therefore, I alternate daily what group of muscles I focus on. I work diligently on stretching and having a flexible muscle mass. Everything I do is focused on maintaining a healthy body. From trying to get 8-10 hours of sleep, to building a powerful core with flexible muscles and joints.

The simple phrase diet and exercise is most applicable to an NFL player as these are world-class athletes who live 24/7 focused on their diet and exercise. Throw in the most complex game books and you see where there is a need for mental alertness and sharpness. Building one's guts, your core, makes you physically strong and mentally powerful.

If there are organized team activities on Monday, it is generally through the watching of film and walk-throughs. This means that we walk through the various plays that we like to run and have organized team conditioning. Even NFL players go through the same types of drills that you see in Pop Warner, high school and collegiate levels. It is all about knowing and learning the basics and conditioning your body for muscle memory and routines.

For example, the greatest power comes from staying low and utilizing leverage. There are speed moves that I utilize in rushing the passer and getting sacks. Repetition is a must.

Monday's film review is from the game the day before. This is where the Kangaroo Courts deliberate, or the team issues fines. The film review can involve an opportunity for the team to bond, as there is much jocularity. However, it is also designed for a learning process to see what good was accomplished and what bad needs to be reconciled.

TUESDAY

The most important day of the week is Tuesday. This is because you can get a jump on the competition. In accordance with NFLPA rules, Tuesdays are a day off for every team in the League. The running of an NFL team is dependent upon one's ability to decipher rules and regulations commensurate with what one would find in a volume of law books.

It is of course, the most popular League and sporting event in the world, and therefore one would assume there are a great many number of rules and regulations that need to be understood. We talked about a team's roster. In addition to that roster, teams are allowed to have practice squad players that actually practice along side the regular roster players during the week.

Practice squad players are players who have hopes and dreams of playing in the NFL, and continue to keep their nose to the grindstone. They feel it an honor and privilege to being part of an NFL organization. Roster players and practice squad players get along very well, and have an appreciation for what one another are doing. From 2008 through 2010, the minimum salary that a practice squad player could receive was $5,200 per week.

For seventeen weeks, that is a minimum of $88,400 per season. For a roster player, the minimum rookie salary for that same time period would be $285,000. For many reasons, the practice squad player hopes to some day be on the roster. More recent figures are $96,900 for a practice squad player, and $390,000 for a rookie salary.

Rules, rules, rules. Whether these are team rules, League rules or Kangaroo Court rules, a player controlling his actions requires a lot of discipline. The NFL and teams provide rules for the manner in which you must wear your socks, to the less stringent of the development of policies. There are rules and then there are polices. Rules relating to how high or low you wear your socks may result in fines and are demands required by the NFL. Policies are issues that are put forth by the NFL that relate to conduct or an honor code that players should attempt to adhere to that relate to the "integrity of the game."

In addition, these polices are ways that the NFL attempts to give us advice on how we can behave in a professional and honorable fashion. For example, believe it or not, the NFL does have policies relating to the providing of sex advice to players. Policies relate to sportsmanship, cooperation with the news media, and guidelines on players endorsing dietary and nutritional supplements, to whether or not players may participate in poker tournaments in gambling establishments. Concerning the sex advice that is provided, there is an AIDS fact sheet, which provides general thoughts and information for a player to consider when involving themselves in sexual relations.

On Tuesday or Wednesday, I will receive a delivery from the NFL via Federal Express that contains the fines that are being assessed against me for the alleged violations of League rules during the previous game. It is not a laughing matter, nor do I enjoy getting letters from the commissioner that takes money from my family and I. On average, I have paid between $30,000-$100,000 a year in fines. I pay these fines with after-tax dollars.

Regardless of what you do for a living, there is the old adage that says, "The more you make the more you spend." Regardless of what you earn, people are tight with their money. We are paid a lot of money; but there is not an unlimited supply. Look at all of the professional athletes, including NFL players who make millions, even tens of millions of dollars, and end up going bankrupt. I hate paying fines and I especially hate that I have to do it with after tax dollars. Most importantly, I do not feel my play on the field justifies NFL fines…most of the time.

When I receive a fine, I do not immediately get my checkbook out to write a check. There is a process for claiming an appeal and working through whether or not the fine should be assessed. Sometimes it is resolved, and not required because I was playing in a manner that does not require a fine, or the amount may be reduced. For example, if someone is flagged during a game for unnecessary roughness, there is a resulting fine. However there are occasions when the NFL reviews the film of the penalty and may have determined that it was not a proper call and therefore, a resulting fine will not be charged. I always review the fines as a process and as part of the game.

One of my favorite coaches, Coach Jim Washburn, once told me "that it is part of doing business in the NFL in that you incur these fines and should see them as being minor in the larger realm of what you are getting paid. Paying these fines is the price you pay to play in a manner where you maximize your potential."

I am not going to slow down or allow the manner in which I play to be inhibited out of the fear of paying a fine. I am all-out chaos, playing at the fastest pace, utilizing the abilities of quickness and power that I have to at its highest potential with extreme violence. Many times I find myself in a situation where a fine is simply not properly assessed. For example, if I get called for a horse collar when the play action is a run/pass option and a zone read, I can engage in a horse collar in the appropriate zone, whereas the League might not see it that way. Who is right? Generally, I am. But the League gets their fine.

Tuesday is a mandatory off day according to the rules, but most players go to the training facility to workout. They also go there to treat injuries and get a jump on the competition by reviewing film for the upcoming game.

WEDNESDAY

The most important day of the week is Wednesday because it is the actual first day of game week. I continue in the weight room and weight lifting as a continuation of what I did on Monday. Tuesday's workout focused on different muscle groups. Hopefully by Wednesday I am feeling much better and continue to have a great workout.

The first day of a new game week is the institution of fresh game plans and the review of scouting reports. Again, there are breakdowns into positions and there is the institution of what we will be doing in the upcoming game, and how we will install those schemes and plays. We have the opportunity to review what our scouts have indicated we can expect from the upcoming opposing team.

Wednesday and Thursday are similar in that, early morning, we break into offensive and defensive group meetings. Later in the morning we have walk throughs to see what we will be installing and walking through as a team. This brings us to lunch around 12:30-1 p.m. In the middle of the day around lunchtime, there is media access to the team. After the lunch and brief media access, by mid-afternoon around 2 p.m. we will have a practice that will go until around 5 p.m. Wednesday is generally a long day with a focus on shifting from what we did the week before, to the new game plan.

THURSDAY

Thursday is the most important day of the week because the installation of the new game plan has taken place the day before, and this is the first opportunity that we have to run the game situations out on the practice field. This is the first time we are working on the development and installation to the running of what we will see and do on the upcoming Sunday. We produce and finish third downs, and get off the field or stop their gaining first downs on their third downs and getting possession of the ball back.

Third down conversions include gaining them and stopping them. Thursday is a long day in running through all of the game situations that we are going to engage on Sunday, and expect from the opponent. There is a lot of film study regarding what we can expect from the opponent and how we plan on playing against specific situations. There is also the run-through for kick off and kick returns. The game plan is set and worked through on the field. Thursday is a long, long day.

FRIDAY

Friday is the most important day of the week because the players must perfect specific game situations. Both sides of the ball, defense and offense, install and practice our red zone game plan, and run through the two-minute drill. The core team breakdowns (punt, punt return, kickoff and kick return) are reviewed. As a team, we will review "exotics" and the point after touchdowns, field goals and onside kicks.

Friday is also the most important day of the week because the practice should be clean, precise, and should move along with a very limited amount of corrections. The players are on and are making pretty much their last organized efforts toward winning the game on Sunday. Friday is a long, long day. However, it is generally, as far as time measurements go, not as late of a day as Wednesday or Thursday.

SATURDAY

Saturday is the most important day of the week as it is your last opportunity to make sure that you have everything done, and done right, before the Sunday kickoff. Whether the upcoming game is home or away, Saturday commences early in the morning. The early start begins with team meetings, game plans and film review. It is important at this point that all of the players understand the game plan and the plays are done without requiring thought.

The NFL is the highest velocity game of speed and quickness, both in physicality and mental execution. Players have to know where they are supposed to be and what they are supposed to be doing at all times. After the morning meetings, the players are together as a team and walk through the entire game plan. We walk through this plan with shorts, jerseys and no helmets.

It is a complete walk through with absolutely no contact. It covers the entire game plan, offense, defense, kick off, kick return, punt, punt return, point after touchdowns and flea-flickers. The walk-through occurs very rapidly and in a precise manner.

The entire process is around one hour. At this point we are prepared to either head to the hotel for a home game or to the airport for an away game. Arrival at either destination involves more film review and final meetings in groups and as a team. Finances and logistics. Discipline and routine.

The wheel is created and the cookie- cutter forged as a result of knowing what is best or how a team can put fifty-three men on a roster and perform in a manner that will allow them to win. Human beings are creatures of habit and perform best when they have the opportunity to develop a routine and develop mental reps and physical muscle memory.

Throughout this week, evenings are short and are dedicated to proactive healthcare in the form of muscle and pain management, nutrition and diet, and sleep. We do what you do in the evenings; attempt to have family contact, fun things with friends, and lay on the couch and watch "Modern Family" and "Everybody Loves Raymond". I also enjoy taking in the cultural events in whatever city I may be living in at the time.

Museums relating to artifacts or science and industry are places that I greatly enjoy. In New York, I am an aficionado of Broadway. Jerry Mitchell, a Paw Paw native, has won numerous Tony Awards for his Broadway choreography. It is nice seeing someone from Paw Paw excel on a worldwide level.

I enjoy reading books or surfing the Internet. I have a number of business ventures that require my attention on a daily basis. For example, RedZone Realty Group, that can take care of all your real estate needs (www.redzonerealtygroup.com). Between managing where I live, the family home in Florida and the Ranch in Texas, there is always something that needs attention. I rely heavily on others in the management of what is going on. Without the help of my wife, kids, parents and family and friends, I could not focus on my responsibilities as an NFL football player. There is no "I" in the word "team". Players on a football team rely heavily on each other just like members of a family rely on each other.

It is important to have a routine. Once the routine is down, the player can settle in and focus on winning. Each team gets a "bye week" during the season. I use this week to spend as much time as possible with my family. We love the outdoors, and many times during the year we go to our cattle ranch in Texas. During bye week, we get the opportunity to watch our cows have their babies.

With the weekly schedule being so hectic, whether I am living under the same roof with my family or by myself in another part of the country, we really do not have an opportunity to see each other much during the season. That is the nature of the game. Our sacrifices are nothing compared to what our men and women in the military must endure and the extended periods of time they are away from their loved ones. I after all, am a grown man and am allowed to continue to play a game I have loved since I was a kid.

Chapter Twelve

THEY CALL IT THE OFF SEASON

Really?

There is not an off-season for today's National Football League player. It is a full-time job that includes games, waiting for the next OTA, end of the regular season games, and the NFL playoffs. Thirty-two teams divided into two conferences with sixteen teams each, develop into an exciting bracketed playoff scenario that plays itself out over a course of six to eight weeks. These conferences include:

American Football Conference
Buffalo Bills
New York Jets
New England Patriots
Miami Dolphins
Baltimore Ravens
Pittsburgh Steelers
Cleveland Browns
Cincinnati Bengals
Tennessee Titans
Indianapolis Colts
Houston Texans
Denver Broncos
San Diego Chargers
Oakland Raiders
Kansas City Chiefs
Jacksonville Jaguars

<u>National Football Conference</u>
Dallas Cowboys
Washington Redskins
Philadelphia Eagles
New York Giants
Chicago Bears
Minnesota Vikings
Green Bay Packers
Detroit Lions
Atlanta Falcons
Tampa Bay Buccaneers
New Orleans Saints
Carolina Panthers
Los Angeles Rams
Seattle Seahawks
San Francisco 49ers
Arizona Cardinals

There are just the right amount of teams, pre-season and regular season games, and the proper amount of brackets for an exciting presentation of the playoffs culminating in the Super Bowl.

Just as with the rest of society, players enjoy watching or having an awareness of the developments through the Playoffs and Super Bowl, whether or not we are fortunate enough to be on a team that is participating or not. Just like during the regular season, players on a team get two tickets to each game. In the Super Bowl, the players on each team still only get two free tickets to the game.

Unlike the regular season games, there are not enough tickets to go around for each player to purchase as many as they may want.

Each player on a Super Bowl team can purchase up to thirteen tickets to the game at face value. The amount of tickets they are able to purchase fluctuates from year to year, as well as the face value. On average, most recently, the ticket price was anywhere from $800 to $1,500 per ticket. Therefore, a player could spend $15,000-$20,000 for the maximum amount of tickets he is able to obtain.

It is interesting to see how the NFL distributes Super Bowl tickets among the other teams within the League. Millions of people watch the Super Bowl. It is a desire among many to actually go to the stadium and participate in all the exciting events in person. Thirty-five percent of all available tickets are allotted to each team in the Super Bowl. Each team gets 17.5% of the tickets to the game. Those tickets are divided amongst the players and the front office staff members.

The host team (the team that plays in the stadium that the Super Bowl is played in) are allotted around 6% of the tickets. The other twenty-nine teams in the League are each given 1.2% of the tickets to the game. Most of the other teams that receive their allotted tickets, offer them to players and other members of the organization. Some teams even offer the tickets to season-ticket holders or hold a lottery for their fans. After all of the Super Bowl tickets are distributed among the teams, there is approximately 25% of the tickets distributed to the League. That is quite a large percentage of the available tickets. That is why most people are unable to find them at face value; they simply do not exist.

If you are not fortunate to be on a winning team through the playoffs and make it to the Super Bowl, your head and heart are focused on hopefully having the opportunity next year. NFL players are highly competitive people and really do want to be on winning teams. Each year is a new start, and every player aspires to play in and win a Super Bowl.

The time period between the last play off game and the Super Bowl is two weeks. That middle weekend is when the Pro Bowl is played. It is an honor to be selected to be in the Pro Bowl and it is normally quite a lot of fun to participate in its events. Pro Bowl players are selected among their peers to play the game that generally is a week-long event played in Hawaii.

I have been selected for the Pro Bowl on two occasions. As a defensive end, a statistic that is quite meaningful is my number of sacks. A sack is an opportunity for you to have the ability to showcase and display some of your individual talents of bringing down the quarterback. Many players like to celebrate after making a sack. On a bet, which I lost, after I make a sack, I sometimes do a Mr. Olympia pose. Rushing the passer requires the expenditure of quite a large amount of adrenalin and getting to him before he has released the ball is quite an accomplishment.

Individual statistics however, can be quite deceiving. There have been years when I did not make the Pro Bowl selection because my sack numbers may have been less than when I was selected to the Pro Bowl. However, in my mind, I had more success that year than merely measuring the year in how many sacks I obtained. While the most important thing is to win as a team, the Pro Bowl selection separates that out into individual performance.

Therefore, while on topic, I point out that sometimes statistics are not the best measuring stick for individual performances. The sack statistic is something drawn out as important by the media to the fans. However, there are games where a defensive end may not obtain a sack, but is impacting the game to such an extent that lends itself to a better performance for the team's accomplishment.

After a player's season is over and there are no scheduled games, a player is able to feel a great sense of satisfaction. Hopefully, when the year ends, a player is healthy and has an ability to focus on being on a team next year… and toward a Super Bowl championship. The immediate period after the ending of a season is the opportunity to spend some time with your family and allow your body to recover and recuperate from the grueling season that it just endured.

Just like the business motto of the NFL of finances and logistics, I have tried to put that good business practice in my own affairs. My family's cattle ranch in Texas is a working cattle ranch and needs to, at the very least, pay for itself. It is a profit-driven enterprise. My family and I like to do everything outdoors from fishing, hiking, hunting, boating and swimming. Anything and everything associated with the outdoors is something that we greatly enjoy.

Other than the excitement, we enjoy hunting, which is an exceptional source for our family's food. I require great amounts of protein and I am particularly drawn to maintain good nutrition through lean meats. This includes venison, elk, axis, fallow and upland game birds, which make up a good part of my yearly diet. Our freezers are always full of fresh, natural wild life. Even the beef raised on my cattle ranch provides for a lean and healthy meal.

There is no room for pot bellies in our circles. A little cow manure on one's boot is not cause for a century-long PTSD situation, nor demanding of a hysterical decontamination. Dirt, grime and cow manure is a good day for my family and friends. Doing everything associated with the outdoors demands that we do not allow ourselves to live in a bubble. There are of course risks associated with living such a lifestyle.

Quite regularly on a quad or all-terrain vehicle, someone may get an eyeball scratched by a briar. While hiking, we may step on a ground beehive. That is all part and parcel of living outdoors. Our off season is made up of all-terrain vehicles, guns, chain saws and all the equipment and thrills, frills of running a cattle ranch and running with the bulls.

During this off-season period, while there are a lot of exciting things occurring and a lot of it being done as a family, I am still working full time on my diet, nutrition and musculature development. A lot of football players will allow themselves a "cheat week" where they will eat what ever they decide–double-cheeseburgers with mayo to tons of pizza, pasta, cookies and cake. It is a short-lived experience because it truly reeks havoc on our body. When you treat your body as a temple, the foods that are not good for you actually do cause you to feel ill.

Once nutrition and diet become a lifestyle, the foods you eat become more a matter of routine and habit. There is really not much of a desire to eat foods that you otherwise do not eat because they are not healthy. I will enjoy alcoholic beverages during the holiday seasons. Whether it is Independence Day or Christmas and New Years, there are occasions where I enjoy a cold beer...several cold beers. However, when nutrition and diet are your lifestyle, the realization that alcohol is really a poison to your body and requires effort for your body to process, it is not something that is conducive or productive in trying to maintain the greatest health possible.

Family time and adventure is set amongst a very active workout schedule. Working out is a daily endeavor for me in the off-season. I am constantly trying to build muscle and power. I am constantly working on my quickness, speed and agility. There are many different schools of thought relating to training, and cardiovascular conditioning. Many professional football players have regular weight lifting regimens.

There are old school players like Walter Payton and Herschel Walker, who added spice to the mundane requirement of lifting weights in a regular routine. Herschel Walker's workouts focused on developing core strength. He believed in doing everything to strengthen the core such as push-ups, sit-ups, chin-ups, pull-ups, dips and a lot of quick explosive sprints. Walter Payton had legendary workouts strengthening his core.

He was well known for having running workouts up a hill and in deep sand that were excruciatingly painful and difficult to execute. One of the greatest running backs of all time had one of the most difficult workout routines. Beyond the weight room of reps, reps and more reps, there are many things that a player does to develop their core, agility and speed. It is really a "no days off" lifestyle. It is a constant focus on diet, nutrition and development of muscle, speed and agility. There is no room for getting old, fat or slow. The NFL is all about power and speed.

Another focus for the off season, is your work with other players and our different charitable contributions. Many of us are very involved with charity golf outings or football camps. Most of us are very appreciative of our fans and the lifestyle that they have given us through their enjoyment of the NFL, and we desire to give back.

Today's players are very fortunate compared to those of yesteryear. We do not have to work jobs in the off-season to provide for our families. We are able to focus on being a player. I also like to be engaged with my business affairs. Throughout the season, I have regular meetings with my staff and the off-season allows me more time to be involved with the direction of where our business is going. Regularly, I meet with my manager and publicist and seek to determine ways I can capitalize on my position as a veteran within the NFL.

Players in the 50's and 60's generally held second jobs. It wasn't until the 70's that the players started to earn enough so they did not have to have other employment. In 1963, when the New York Jets drafted Joe Nameth, he was paid $400,000. Today, the average player earns over a million dollars a year. A million dollars per year is a huge difference when compared to the average salary in the 1970's of around $40,000 a year.

Today, a lot of players will get a base salary of $1.5 million dollars. That is quite a lot of money. But imagine a starting quarterback earning between $10-$15 million dollars a year. That is astronomical. The player getting around $1.5 as a base, will generally have the potential for more money each year. That player may get an $850,000 roster bonus. If they play in all sixteen games, they may get a $350,000 bonus. These are all bonuses that are tied to the contract. In addition, they may get a per-game bonus of $21,000. If they are available the following year, they will have an annual roster bonus of around $500,000.

Generally, there are additional incentives such as playtime or sacks of around $775,000. In addition, that contract could be tied to an additional contract that states if they make the roster the following year, they will get a $2.1 million dollar roster bonus on top of the $1 million dollar base, with a $500,000 guaranteed payment. Each player has their own individual contract with incentives and bonuses tied into it. Needless to say, there is a lot of money to be made playing in the National Football League.

Chapter Thirteen

LOVE OF THE GAME
Protecting the Shield

The first organized Player's Association was founded in 1956. It was, and still is, known as the National Football League Player's Association (NFLPA). Since its inception, the NFLPA attempts to provide players with a contract with the owners, known as a Collective Bargaining Agreement (CBA). Essentially, through various strikes and lockouts, the Association is a player's union. The NFLPA is affiliated with the American Foundation of Labor and Congress of Industrial Organizations (AFL-CIO).

As with other areas of commerce, when there are negotiations and disagreements among management and workers/players, there are strikes, lockouts and Federal Anti-Trust Lawsuits. The NFL has seen its fair share of all of the above. The most recent historical CBA's date to an agreement from 1977-1982 resulted in a strike beginning in September 1982. The next CBA lasted until the next strike in 1987.

The 1987, CBA lasted until an Anti-Trust Lawsuit resulted in an actual jury trial in 1989. At the heart of the disputes and class-action lawsuit brought by Reggie White, was free agency and salary cap terms. During this time, lawsuits dominated how the League would resolve player disputes until 1993 Agreements. The 1993 settlements were extended five times, with the final extension covering 2006 through the 2010 season.

I was a player representative for the Tennessee Titans for the 2011 CBA negotiations. In my opinion, the players were happy with the existing CBA and wanted to continue and extend its terms. The owners chose to lock us out. Money. Money. Money. The NFL is the pinnacle in sports leagues and entertainment in sports on this planet. There is no other event more popular or that draws more televisions spectators. The television dollars are enormous. Unions, management, ownership, and money has (since the beginning of civilization) caused friction and disagreements within human interactions.

How is the money divided in any business amongst ownership and labor? It is not just money. It is billions and billions of dollars. Many believe that the current CBA shifts billions of dollars from the players to the owners. Other issues relate to the length of the season, how many pre-season and regular season games we have. If the players argue for less pre-season games, the owners will agree as long as there are more regular season games. Once the owners got to twenty games, it isn't going down.

While the players were focused on doing away with two-a-day and full contact practices in a long drawn out pre-season, the owners blind-sided them with four pre-season games as a trade off. It was a blind-side as it got the owners to the 20; a realization that occurred later while the players thought they accomplished something by getting the less harsher practice schedule.

Bargaining chips include long-term health care for retired players and types of pensions. Every side has its position regarding the true revenue realized and profitability in the League. The work we did in 2011 provides a CBA that is supposed to run through 2020. With millions, billions at stake, who is to say that the owners will not impose another work stoppage like they did in 2011?

With issues such as players' health benefits, safety concerns, player's salary (veteran scales vs. rookies), team salary caps, television contracts and revenue sharing, free agency issues, training camp and seasonal schedules, nothing is guaranteed. Finances and logistics.

Look at the potential revenue sources–national media revenue, NFL ventures revenue, local club revenue. Now, compare to owners, front office, players and retirees, all wanting their fair share. While the 2011 negotiations were taking place, there was a 44-page Federal Court Class Action lawsuit filed against the League on behalf of former players and retirees. There were lawsuits and billions in television revenue at stake.

The owners were hoping to end with an agreement with them getting, for starts, one billion dollars off the top of all revenue. Nice starting point, for them. They will make up the costs to them, by adding two more games to the regular season…not so fast. Easy for them, but quite a different story for an athlete trying to maintain their physical condition through a long enough season as it is.

In the end, they didn't get their billion, but they got out of paying $320 million in benefits for an uncapped year and no judicial oversights in disputes between players and owners and settlement of all pending litigation. (There were numerous suits.) The dispute resolution issue seems to have dominated the media and fan interest the most, with the elevation of Commissioner Goodell to the heights of Supreme, Royal Commander as judge, jury and executioner, Ala Tom Brady, Richie Incognito, Ray Rice, Adrian Peterson, etc., etc., etc.

Giving the Commissioner absolute power is not going to work well...or will it? It just does not make sense. President Abraham Lincoln once said, "Nearly all men can stand adversity, but if you want to test a man's character, give him power." Why cause a person, the Commissioner, to shoulder such a burden? Currently, the Commissioner can make a ruling, then if there is an appeal, that appeal goes back to him.

There is not a system of any kind, throughout the history of mankind (that succeeded) that allowed such absolute power. However, the NFL is not a government trying to manage a civilization. It is a business.

What is reasonable? Should the Commissioner's decision appeal to a panel consisting of three representatives–one from the League, one from the players, and one that those two mutually select? Tell me you are not now nodding your head in agreement? Or are you shaking your head saying, "That is not how a business is run."

The players won 55% percent of national television and media revenue, 45% percent of all NFL ventures, and 40% of local club revenue; including one billion dollars in additional benefits for retired players and an opportunity for retirees to stay in the player's medical plan for life. A sixteen-game schedule, fewer weeks of OTAs, elimination of two-a-day practices in pads, limited full contact practices, an unrestricted free agency after four years also were part of the agreement.

The estimated yearly value of the CBA is $12-16 billion dollars a year. The issues addressed thus far, are really just the tip of the iceberg. Imagine all of the issues that arise when tens of billions of dollars are at stake, and throw in some of the brightest business minds our economy has to offer and you can understand the effort and sacrifices made by players to be a part of it all. I have never thought of it as much as a career as I have thought of being in the NFL as an opportunity. It is an opportunity that is more than just a job, while you have a spot in it; it is a lifestyle and a commitment worth making to hold onto the opportunity with a deep sense of appreciation.

My concern for the League's future is whether or not all of the sides (meaning the owners) understand that it is an opportunity for all of those involved. Rotary International has a test for the appropriateness of negotiations and agreements. It is known as the Rotary four-way test. First, is it the truth? Second, is it fair to all concerned? Third, will it build good will and better friendships? Fourth, will it be beneficial to all concerned? An agreement that fairly addresses all four of these issues is sound in its four corners. Something different than that and akin to what the owners are sometimes accused of, begs the expression, "pigs get fat and hogs get slaughtered."

In light of what the League seems to really be concerned about, they should concern themselves with the hog adage and what the future holds for the League. Developing franchise and transition tags, along with a rookie wage system with a no-opt-out clause for players that have over ten years, clearly shows what the owners are really interested in (obviously money). Again, we always have to keep in mind that it is a business. It is also clear the route they plan to take to get it–cheap labor, without a concern for the veteran player who provides quality to the game.

Can the NFL possibly collapse when it fields players based on economics and not performance? It used to be that a veteran was terminated because he was no longer as good of a performer as someone else. What happens when cheap labor overtakes the League and supplants quality players? Now veterans are cut because they can be replaced with a cheaper–not necessarily a better player. It is a brutal cycle; but that is the way it is. This only heightens ones appreciation for being able to be a part of it.

Another financial motivation for a team to release a veteran is something the players actually negotiated, thinking it would be a benefit for them. However, this has surely backfired. The thought was that if a veteran was cut after a season started, after the first game, the player could claim termination pay from that team. This is a benefit that can only be claimed once. The intention was to provide some guaranteed money to a player who earned it from the many years in the League.

The eligibility threshold is four years; but remember, the average NFL career spans three years. The amount of the pay is based on a formula from the player's existing contract. When the pay is utilized under the situation it was designed for, it is a fair attempt at balancing the two competing interests. After a deal is in place for a few years the loopholes start to develop like a head of Wisconsin Cheese.

My grandfather was involved in Unions in Chicago, and I tried to help as a player representative for the 2011 CBA, so I am not a babe in the woods when it comes to understanding management and labor. It is important to note however, that the NFL is not working on a shoestring budget and it needs to be careful with how it develops and maintains its level of action. Veterans need to be evaluated on their level of performance and not on how much money can be saved if they are cut. There is a reason they get paid more; because they have proven they can play.

What sense does it make to take someone with proven talent and a proven caliber of play, and remove them simply based on the perception that their compensation no longer fits the team's finances? Finances and logistics. Duh. Ironically, what was negotiated as a benefit for the veterans has hurt those that have the talent and ability to continue playing after they passed a team's threshold of what their financial worth has become.

Watch for the large number of veterans cut the day before the fifty-three-man roster deadline, who, throughout camp were a lock to make the team. Unfortunately, the good of the league cannot be blinded with individual concerns. Lots of players want in, but few get a chance. These types of cuts will undoubtedly have a negative effect on the level of future performance, level of play, and the overall health of the NFL. Sure, there will always be marquee players; television revenue demands it. However, can marquee players last or even develop when surrounded by sub-par labor? What good is window dressing without a window?

In the 1970's, marquee players forced ownership's hand and left the NFL for a bigger paycheck in the World Football League (WFL). How long did the World Football League last trying to rely only on marquee players? They didn't last long at all. The best League fields the best players. A consequence of the post 2011 CBA is that the NFL is infusing the League with cheap labor and casting away the highest caliber veterans if they are not seen as marquee or worthy of a fair paycheck.

The base line salary cap for each of the NFL teams is $143 million dollars. The cap is determined by reviewing the amount of Defined Gross Revenue (DGR) each team receives. The DGR is determined through a formula considering National Television Revenue, ticket sales, NFL merchandise sales, naming rights and local advertising.

Consider minimum rookie salaries, signing bonuses, back-loaded contracts, contracts that are not guaranteed, cap-friendly contracts, heavy payloads, transition players and franchise players. Show me someone who says they really understand all of this, and I will show you someone who doesn't know what they are talking about; or has developed their own little loopholes under such a system. In such a system, the prevailing mode of operation is circumvention.

Rules that are so flim-flammy are easily maneuvered.

Some players make millions of dollars a year. Fans hear about a marquee player getting $10 million dollars a year. Even the NFL minimum salary schedule involves a lot of money.

Years in the League	2015	2016	2017	2018
0	$435,000	$450,000	$465,000	$480,000
1	$510,000	$525,000	$540,000	$555,000
2	$585,000	$600,000	$615,000	$630,000
3	$660,000	$675,000	$690,000	$705,000
4-6	$745,000	$760,000	$775,000	$790,000
7-9	$870,000	$885,000	$900,000	$915,000
10+	$970,000	$985,000	$1,000,000	$1,015,000

There is a team that is actually valued at $4 billion dollars and has a quarterback contract worth $100 million dollars. Talk about diversity and trying to figure out the best business model to get to the Super Bowl. Hubris leaders, Draconian methods and rulings–how can such a League last? Easy. It is a business, so run it like a business.

For instance, teams with heavy payloads learn the best way to comply with the salary cap is to circumvent it. What? Push the large money owed to a player to the end of their contract and when the remaining years arrive, cut the player. Again, the level of performance goes down when the player is released for cheap labor. There are around 1,600 slots that millions want to fill. This may be counteracted, for marquee players with the ability to pay signing bonuses.

Now we have come full circle back to the relevance of media hype around key players. And what happens to a League that is striving for excellence, but relies on flash and glitz players surrounded by sub-par talent? The level of performance will continue to go down. How is there equal bargaining or negotiations or concern for a four-way test when the owners have a $4 billion lockout war chest. When will the system go bust? It won't.

In addition, with the competition to fill the limited number of slots, it will always be entertaining and highly competitive. Wear pink shoes, socks, gloves…fight cancer–a very worthy cause. Add a woman to the coaching staff. Have a female referee. All legitimate, altruistic endeavors being more inclusive. Of course, what would one expect from the greatest League ever, with maintaining the highest protocols and standards among businesses within our modern society. Such moves will expand the market and increase revenue.

Does a fan base get turned off by such behavior? Does the ability to have exponential growth fizzle out, or run dry? It is, after all, all about the fans. Between players and owners, it is a constant battle over who has the leverage with the fans. Is it possible for the fans to not want to watch something just because it is football? Whatever happened to the WFL? The USFL? And how healthy is arena football?

Pay attention to a NFL team with a star marquee quarterback making $5-10 million dollars a year that starts the season 0-2 then

0-3. Changes are soon made to the offensive line and the defense. You cannot expect to succeed with a marquee player surrounded by cheap labor. Rebuilding years don't cut it anymore.
Everyone wants to win now.

We cannot just stand by and watch the best of the best fall by the wayside. Someone needs to act, and we rely upon sports media (i.e., Fox Sports or ESPN) to analyze and address the issue. We will not see them reporting on the affects of exclusionary overrides and the League's reliance upon cheap, disposable labor. In 2014, we saw approximately 160 players come out of the college ranks early. That is a huge influx of labor in addition to the normal incoming rookies. The fierce competition certainly makes the action explosive.

I bring this discussion to the forefront because I care about the League's future, and love the game. I am grateful to the fans and my teammates and would feel remiss and a failure if I did not sound the alarms. I am not even talking about the fans getting sick and tired of what the game is becoming.

No more big hits, big plays, big kick returns, big blocks, big pass receptions called back, big plays missed all together because they occur during television commercials. In 2015, the owners tried to actually make the game more exciting by moving back the point after touchdown. It is now a field goal kick from the 15-yard line. Big hits swapped out with a longer PAT.

Wow! The owners didn't push for the eighteen-game schedule, or more games during the 2011 CBA negotiations because fan polls showed that most fans did not want a longer season. While the NFL is King, when does too much of a great thing just become too much? These concerns do go hand in hand with what I am worried about; an entire systemic examination–or termination.

The concerns I have are founded in the reasoning of people like Dallas Maverick owner Mark Cubin, when they predict that the NFL will implode within the next ten years. Am I not protecting and honoring the shield by sounding the alarms. Cubin, has said "I think the NFL is ten years away from an implosion. When pigs get fat, hogs get slaughtered and they're getting hoggy. When you try to take it too far, people turn the other way.

I am just telling you, when you got a good thing and you get

greedy, it always, always, always, always, always turns against you."
Expanding the market and TV saturation, coupled with player behavior and performance, forms the foundation of his opinions. It is
for my love of the game, the fans and hope for the future health of the
League that I bring this to your attention.

Chapter Fourteen

WHO IS THE STOOGE?

The game of football has come a long way from when it was first played. The rules, equipment and millions of other nuances have changed. The playing of the sport professionally in organized leagues originated in Ohio. The NFL Hall of Fame is in Canton, Ohio, as that is where the roots of today's League started its growth.

Many of the eras find their differences in some rather general rule changes. For instance, there are obvious regulation changes such as the size and shape of the football. It went from the heavy watermelon from yesteryear to the modern aerial rocket. Such changes are going from opening up the passing game, to extending the height of the goal posts by five feet.

A controversial call in a game between the Patriots and the Ravens, led to a push for taller uprights. Kicks that go above the post top cannot be reviewed, and whether the kick puts points on the scoreboard (if it is high) can be difficult to discern.

Equipment rules clearly affect the way the game is played. Football shapes, size, and air pressure to the height of goal posts, the use of helmets, and the materials used to make them have evolved. Regulations affect the way the game is played and also changes how players play. Some refer to the Golden Age of Football being between the 1970's and 1990's. Big hits. Big runs. Big plays.

Compared to the "golden age", players cannot hit the quarterback above the shoulders, or below the waist. And receivers cannot be touched after the first five yards. Clearly, the passing game is wide open now, making today's game much more conducive to quarterbacks and receivers. Yet, even with these rules that some feel have taken away the violence and excitement from the game, it remains at its highest levels of popularity with the fans, media, and general public at large.

Has the game changed for the better? Has the League become better at managing its entertainment value to the public and its fans? Do rules prohibiting players from using face paint during a game make the sport more popular? (Really–there have been fines for

$7,500 against NFL players for wearing face paint).

How does it help the League and the game's popularity to fine Pete Carroll, head coach of the Seattle Seahawks, personally, $100,000 for running a mini-camp in June that had excessive contact between the players? The penalties include a $200,000 fine in addition against the team and it will lose two mini-camp practices next season.

One of the most confusing aspects of the NFL is the application of its fine system. It is a Tyrannical system, run by Commissioner Goodell, with a goal to please the media and the fans. Attempts at swaying public opinion to its favor over the players and coaches, causes a constant drawing and re-drafting of the battle lines. It causes a rift between those who play the game and those who take the money and negatively affect how the teams compete and try to win games.

While the League has an established list of infractions and the amounts of fines associated with a first and second offense, most people, including the players, do not have any knowledge or understanding of how the system operates. Since the 2011 CBA, Article 46, Section 1D of the CBA states: "the 2011 schedule of fines, which has been provided to and accepted by the NFLPA shall serve as the basis of discipline for the infractions identified on that schedule." Further, within Section 1D, it states: "the designated minimum fine amounts will increase by five percent for the 2012 League year, and each League year thereafter during the terms of this Agreement."

The CBA states that the Commissioner has the discretion and ability to impose fines outside of the fine schedule "where circumstances warrant, including, but not limited to, the infractions that were flagrant and gratuitous, larger fines, suspension or other discipline may be imposed."

Following the 2011 CBA, it was stated by Commissioner Goodell, that his authority in enforcing and policing the integrity of the game gives him the widest, broadest powers imagined in protecting player safety.

It states: "The Commissioner may impose fines and other appropriate discipline, up to and including suspension or banishment from the League, for certain misconduct on the playing field, as well as for conduct detrimental to the integrity of or public confidence in the NFL or the game of professional football."

Further: "A player who is a repeat offender should expect game suspensions and beyond in the same season or based on prior season violations will be established on a case-by-case basis and may increase substantially."

The League has further established through the CBA language itself that fines are not only subject as a result of fouls called by game officials during the game. "Discipline is not based solely on situations where game officials call fouls. In some cases, a violation may be detected in post-game review of video."

Usually fines can also follow certain penalties, from either the NFL or from the team or from the player Kangaroo Court. Sometimes just because a flag is thrown, it does not mean that a fine is automatic. The NFL does review the film before assessing the fine. There are the rare occasions they find the flag was not appropriate, or they may find that the penalty was sufficient.

The 2012 fine schedule is as follows (add 5% each additional year, compounded annually to the present to determine present day values):

Fine Type:	$ 1st min.	$2nd min.
Striking/ Kicking/ Kneeing	$7,875	$15,750
Horse Collar Tackle	$15,750	$31,500
Face Mask	$7,875	$15,750
Leg Whip	$15,750	$31,500
Late Hit	$7,875	$15,750

Spearing	$21,000	$42,000
Impermissible Use of Helmet	$21,000	$42,000
Hit on Defenseless Player	$21,000	$42,000
Blindside Block	$21,000	$42,000
Roughing the Passer	$15,750	$31,500
Low Block	$7,875	$15,750
Chop Block	$7,875	$15,750
Fighting	$26,500	$52,500
Entering Fight Area (active)	$5,250	$10,500
Entering Fight Area (inactive)	$2,625	$7,875
Unsportsmanlike Conduct	$10,500	$21,000
Taunting	$7,875	$10,500
Football into Stands	$5,250	$10,500
Foreign Substance	$7,875	$15,750
Chin Straps	$7,875	$10,500

Personal Messages	$5,250	$10,500
Uniform/Equipment Violation	$5,250	$10,500
Physical Contact with Official	$26,250	$52,500
Verbal/Non-Physical Offense Against Official	$21,000	$42,000

NFL penalties are as follows:

*Penalties that result in an Automatic First Down
(Awarded to Offensive Team on All Defensive Fouls
with these Exceptions):*

Offside
Encroachment
Delay of Game
Illegal Substitution
Excessive time out(s)
Incidental grasp of face mask
Neutral zone infraction
Running into the kicker
More than 11 players on the field at the snap

Penalties that result in Five Yards
(Awarded against the team that committed the penalty)

Defensive holding or illegal use of hands
Delay of game on offense or defense
Delay of kickoff
Encroachment Excessive time out(s) False start
Illegal formation/Illegal Shift
Illegal Motion
Illegal Substitution
First onside kickoff out of bounds between goal lines and untouched or last touched by kicker
Invalid fair catch signal
More than 11 players on the field at snap for either team
Less than seven men on offensive line at snap
Offside
Failure to pause one second after shift or huddle
Running into kicker
More than one man in motion at snap
Grasping facemask of the ball carrier or quarterback
Player out of bounds at snap
Ineligible member(s) of kicking team going beyond line of scrimmage before ball is kicked
Illegal return
Failure to report change of eligibility
Neutral zone infraction
Loss of team time out(s) or five-yard penalty on the defense for excessive crowd noise
Ineligible player downfield during passing down
Second forward pass behind the line
Forward pass is first touched by eligible receiver who has gone out of bounds and returned
Forward pass touches or is caught by an ineligible receiver on or behind line
Forward pass thrown from behind line of scrimmage after ball once crossed the line
Kicking team player voluntarily out of bounds during a punt

Twelve (12) men in the huddle
Penalties that result in Ten Yards
(Awarded against the team that committed the penalty)

Offensive pass interference
Holding, illegal use of hands, arms or body by offense
Tripping by a member of either team
Helping the runner
Deliberately batting or punching a loose ball
Deliberately kicking a loose ball
Illegal block above the waist

Penalties that result in Fifteen Yards
(Awarded against the team that committed the penalty)

Chop block
Clipping below the waist
Fair catch interference
Illegal crack back block by offense
Piling on
Roughing the kicker
Roughing the passer
Twisting, turning or pulling an opponent by the face mask
Unnecessary roughness
Unsportsmanlike conduct
Delay of game at start of either half
Illegal low block
A tackler using his helmet to butt, spear or ram an opponent
Any player who uses the top of his helmet unnecessarily
A punter, placekicker, or holder who simulates being roughed by
a defensive player
Leaping
Leverage
Any player who removes his helmet after a play while on the field
Taunting

Other Penalties
Five yards and loss of down (combination penalty)
Forward pass thrown from beyond the line of scrimmage

10 Yards and Loss of Down (combination penalty)

Intentional grounding of forward pass (safety if passer is in own end zone) (if foul occurs more than 10 yards behind line, play results in loss of down at spot of foul)
15 Yards and Loss of Coin Toss Option
Team's late arrival on the field prior to scheduled kickoff
Captains not appearing for coin toss
15 Yards (and disqualification if flagrant) striking opponent with fist
Kicking or kneeing opponent
Striking opponent on head or neck with forearm, elbow, or hands whether or not the initial contact is made below the neck area
Roughing kicker
Roughing passer
Malicious unnecessary roughness
Unsportsmanlike conduct
Palpably unfair act (distance penalty determined by referee after consultation with other officials)

15 Yards and Automatic Disqualification
Using a helmet (not worn) as a weapon
Striking or purposely shoving a game official Suspension From Game for One Down
Illegal equipment (player may return after one down when legally equipped) Touchdown awarded (palpably unfair act) when referee determines a palpably unfair act deprived a team of a touchdown.

The average play takes 5-7 seconds in the NFL.
Here is an example of just one play:

The players transition out of the last pile up rather smoothly. There is no name-calling or exchanges of hostile unpleasantness. Little did Curly realize that the opponents QB, Larry, managed to pull one of Curly's socks down to his ankle as Curly used Larry's head as leverage to assist him in raising his 350 pound body to his feet.

It was now 3rd and 4 on Larry's 45. A moment before the ball was snapped Curly had crossed the line of scrimmage on a mission of sacking Larry before he could throw for first down. Larry's teammates (ever so aware of Curly's rushing abilities) assigned two blockers to the task of keeping him at bay. Curly's teammate down the line, Moe, recognizing the offensive tactics taken towards Curly, allowed him to make a stunt inside Curly's planned path of attack.

Just as Moe was going to lay Larry out, Larry was holding the ball in a manner as though he was going to attempt to pass it forward; in a split second, Moe nailed Larry and drove him to the ground. The ball disappeared between the legs of several men from both teams.

Was Larry intentionally moving his arm forward in an attempt to complete a forward pass when he lost possession of the ball as Moe hit him and drug him to the ground by the nape of his neck and shoulder pads? Or, did Larry lose possession of the ball as he was attempting to tuck it back towards his body?

In the first scenario, when the ball hits the ground, it is an incomplete pass. Under the later circumstance, it is a fumble; under the tuck rule, which existed in the NFL from 1999 to 2013, if the QB drops or loses possession of the football while he is bringing the ball forward as though he is passing the ball but then changes his mind and tries to keep the ball, tucking it into his body, rather than throwing the ball, it is still considered a forward pass and not a fumble. But it's an incomplete pass when the ball hits the ground.

Was Larry's arm moving forward because he was throwing the ball, or was his arm moving forward because of Moe's 350 pound body and force of immeasurable velocity and power drove Larry's arm forward causing the ball to tumble to the ground? Was Larry's intent to throw the ball down field for a first down, or tuck it to his body in preparation for getting smoked by Moe? Answer that, and you can tell what I am thinking at the very moment that you are reading this…not when I wrote it.

The NFL finally eliminated the tuck rule in 2013, but even without it, seldom is the call a fumble or incomplete pass an entirely easy call. Even after minutes of review by replay officials, the controversy arises in a situation that can mean the difference of winning or losing, advancing in the playoffs or ending your season. Seldom is there unanimous agreement on whether it was a fumble or incomplete pass. At least an option of whether it was a tuck still doesn't exist. However, in actuality, it still comes down to the question of whether it was a fumble or pass. The tuck rule, however, was just another rule helping the QB's.

As Larry, Moe and Curly scrum for the ball with all of the other players, quite a pile up ensued. As Festus wrapped his big mitts around the ball, Grover jumped upon the ball covering it with his stomach. Festus and Grover let out the loudest grunts, growls, and gut yelps as they fought against each other to claim complete possession of the ball, each had several players from the other teams pulling and yanking at every part of their body trying to claim sole possession.

The men claw, yank, scratch, and punch-no holds barred. This could be the play that decides the game. Sixty minutes of regulation decided in seconds. Both men felt fingers the size of sausages poking at their eyes and tugging on their nose as attempts were made at getting a fishhook to land.

Just as Grover thought he could roll out of the pile with the ball, he was put on the receiving end of a perfectly executed oil check. The deeply penetrating finger bang caused Grover to be distracted with both mental engagement and body sensation such that he lost the intensity necessary to roll out with possession of the ball. At the moment of Grover's bolt away from the oil check, Festus was able to pull the ball out and claim it as a turn over and effectuate the much-needed change of possession.

Further review would confirm Larry was not flailing his arm forward in a passing motion. Rather, he was merely driven by the forces brought forth by Moe. It was a fumble, recovered by Festus, and

Curly, Moe and the rest of the team could not be more jubilant. Calls through laughter to their opponents, calling into question their true manhood or what their mothers did last night, or on a regular basis were soon drowned out by the visions of the yellow handkerchief laying not too far off from the original line of scrimmage.

Curly was off sides! No change of possession-no fumble recovery. Larry's team gets a first down. Larry's team then goes on to win the game. Curly's off sides cost his team the game. Or, was it really just a split second among 3,600 seconds? A few days later, Curly will get a Federal Express package from the NFL fining him for that one play. Horse collar $17,000, roughing the passer $17,000, socks around his ankle $3,000.

The next day, his teammates will also assess him for an off sides penalty and negating a change of possession in the amount of $2,000. Curly was, as he was ever so often found, scratching his head and appealed his NFL fines. How could he be fined for roughing the passer when there was no flag for roughing the passer? Curly will appeal the NFL fines, but there is no appeal of his teammates decision.

The NFL will retract the horse collar, given where it took place and the QB's movements (that's why it wasn't flagged-duh). Sometimes, even if it results in a flag, it does not necessarily mean there will be fines. Sometimes there is no flag, but there are fines. The eye gouges, fishhooks and oil check all go by as events that did not take place because they happened at the bottom of the pile and went unseen.

Even though there are eyes in the sky and cameras at every angle on an NFL field, not everything is seen. Larry is happy the referee didn't hear him call him a Nimrod for not calling roughing the passer and he therefore, won't be hit with a $25,000 fine. With a specific, spelled-out fine schedule, it seems most fines are self-explanatory. However, the NFL has made it clear that discipline will be on a case-by-case basis.

Evaluations will occur on its own facts and circumstances, including most importantly it seems to the NFL, whether or not the infraction occurred "during the normal course of the game" versus "outside the normal course of the game." Within the course of a game, is when a situation is consistent with the competitive tempo, pace and situation or compared to outside being flagrant, unnecessary, avoidable or gratuitous. All of this decision-making is subjective on the part of the NFL decision makers.

The fining system is another means that the NFL uses to raise revenue. However, the NFL states that it is not a revenue source. Obviously the NFL is able to say what it is or isn't, and it will state for many reasons, that it is not a revenue source so that it will not become subject to sharing with the CBA. The NFL states that all of the fines against coaches and players are either donated to charity or used to support the NFL's retired players; donations that in other types of business enterprises, result from taking money from its revenue.

The fine system is clearly in place as a means of trying to establish uniformity. Whether it is in how the player's appear or how they behave. All of this has, as an underlying motivation, the concern for how the product is able to be marketed to the general public, the fans and the media.

As a player, I honor and cherish the fans. It is to them, that I am indebted to for allowing such a prestigious League to exist and thrive. It is with great satisfaction that we have a fan base that is sophisticated enough to overcome the bias and sloppy reporting by the current environment of today's media.

There seems to be a constant battle between the League and players as to who has the leverage with the fans and media. Is the battle with those who charge $10 for a hot dog, those who build nice fancy stadiums, or those who create commercial time outs for squeezing the television dollars through Thursday and Saturday football games after the college season is over?

Unfortunately, the participants in today's media are not the Al Michaels, Frank Gifford's and Don Meredith's of their time. There are way too many that have not earned their stripes. The last ten years has seen an enormous change in the numbers of media outlets reporting on sports. How many channels does ESPN have now? Fox Sports? The NFL has its own network. There are not enough of those in the media that have earned their stripes such as a Steven A. Smith, Mike Greenberg, Mike Golic or Jay Glazer.

We use to have sources in the media give any attention to events such as Wide World of Sports or Monday Night Football. Now, with ESPN and Fox Sports, there is a constant 24/7 media surge and buzz. There is literally ESPN's "Up All Night" on both radio and television. After a game, all I want to do is get out of my clothes and replenish my body with liquids, carbs, and protein.

Most players are completely spent after a game. There is nothing left in the tank. Can you imagine standing by your locker, naked, after a loss, being asked: "Why couldn't your defense stop their running game?"

"Ahhh... because we didn't tackle the guy with the ball..."

We play the game to win. Generally, the opponent is just who we thought they were. We are trying to win the game and it does not help at the end of the game to try to answer questions about why we did not win the game and how and what changes we will make next week, when all the player wants to do is finish getting undressed, get in the shower and get something to eat. But with the 24/7 news outlets, there is a constant need for information and an unlimited supply of those out trying to obtain it.

Is it too much to ask that "some" in the media should do their homework before asking questions and printing stories? If a lame-brain question is asked and you feel you know what the politically correct answer is, please do not include the politically incorrect answer in the wording that is expressed in posing the question. I am trying to play the game I love and provide entertainment to deserving fans and do not understand why I should be fodder for your attempts at providing salacious information.

Sometimes a player even wonders if a reporter understands the game with the type of question they ask. For example, a pass-rusher was trying to get to the quarterback. Success is not only measured by whether the player can tackle the quarterback while he still has the ball (a sack). But, success is measured by whether or not the rusher is able to force the quarterback to get rid of the ball before he desires to throw it, and have an unsuccessful scramble.

Media criticism for a lack of sacks, totally fails to understand the role and achievement and successes of a pass-rusher that may lack the sack count that the reporter deems meritorious. Ten years ago, there were not the opinion shows, sport shows or bloggers writing about issues that simply do not make sense. There has been a dramatic change in sports reporting. There are reporters who work in that arena who have not earned their "stripes", but act as a participant in the world's most elite League.

Diametrically, at the other end of the spectrum, are those veteran reporters who provide an entertaining and informative broadcast of what is happening in a game and around the League. I think a consequence of the competition among the media is that you see a lot of female reporters who work hard and are prepared to understand the game; adding a refreshingly positive view on the sport.

The world's most prestigious and popular sporting event includes some of the most fascinating players from League officials, owners, managers and players, to the most important participant– you the fan. It is through your critique that the commissioner feels the heat of inconsistent rulings or as to what rules will be allowed. It is through your support that the player continues his love for the game. It is through your voice that it is determined whether or not the market is being saturated or that you continue to be hungry for the game and the League.

It is up to you to determine the future of the National Football League and how its history will have been understood. It is through your important place in what happens on the gridiron and in the game I love, that this book is dedicated to you, the fans.

Thank you!

ABOUT THE AUTHORS

Jason Babin is a native of Paw Paw, Michigan where he was a star athlete at Paw Paw High School; being selected for state honors in football, wrestling, and track and field. He attended Western Michigan University and played for the university's Bronco Football team where he was recognized as first-team and second-team All American honors by the NFL Draft Report College Record, and *Sports Illustrated* respectively.

After graduation, he was a first-round draft pick for the Houston Texans where he played from 2004-06. He went on to play for the Seattle Seahawks (2007-08), Kansas City Chiefs (2008), Philadelphia Eagles (2009), Tennessee Titans (2010), Philadelphia Eagles (2011-12), Jacksonville Jaguars (2013), New York Jets (2014), the Baltimore Ravens (2015), and the Arizona Cardinals (2015). He currently lives in Florida with his wife and children.

Matthew R. Cooper made national headlines and has been featured in *The New York Times*, and on various media such as the *CBS Evening News* and *National Public Radio,* for his role as the lead litigator in the landmark Hurley Case. He represented U.S. Army Sgt. James Hurley, an Iraq War Veteran from Hartford, Michigan, whose home was illegally foreclosed as he served in Iraq.

Cooper helped Hurley in a battle against Wall Street that would forever protect the rights of all personnel serving in the United States Military. It resulted in millions of dollars in retribution paid to soldiers by banks due to illegal foreclosure during their active duty service in battle. His actions effectuated amendments by Congress to the Servicemembers' Civil Relief Act. The court case resulted in Cooper's debut book, *A Soldier's Home: United States Servicemembers vs. Wall Street.*

He graduated cum laude from Western Michigan University with a bachelor's degree in public administration and political science, and received his JD from Valperasio University School of Law in Indiana. He currently has a law office in Paw Paw, Michigan and serves as chairman of the Servicemembers Civil Relief Act Foundation.